Plan of Garden in a Valley

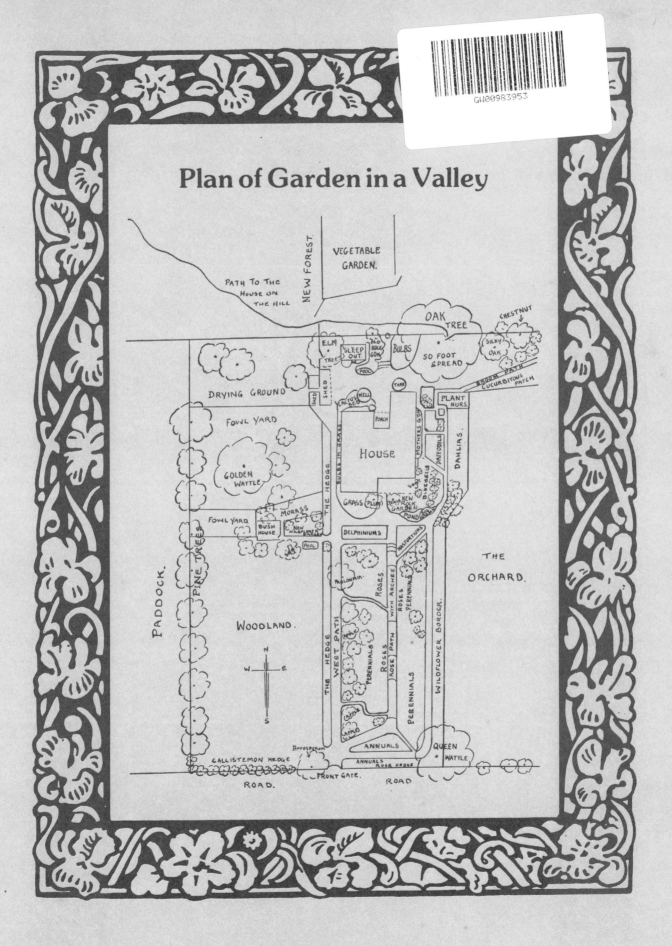

GARDEN
in a
VALLEY

Dedication

To the Two at home who lived the garden story,
and John Inglis Lothian who encouraged it.

> If the hid and sealed coffer
> Whose having not his is,
> To the loosers may proffer
> Their finding—here this is;
> Their lives, if all livers
> To the Life of all living
> To you, O dear givers,
> I give your own giving.
>
> Francis Thompson

GARDEN
in a
VALLEY

Jean Galbraith

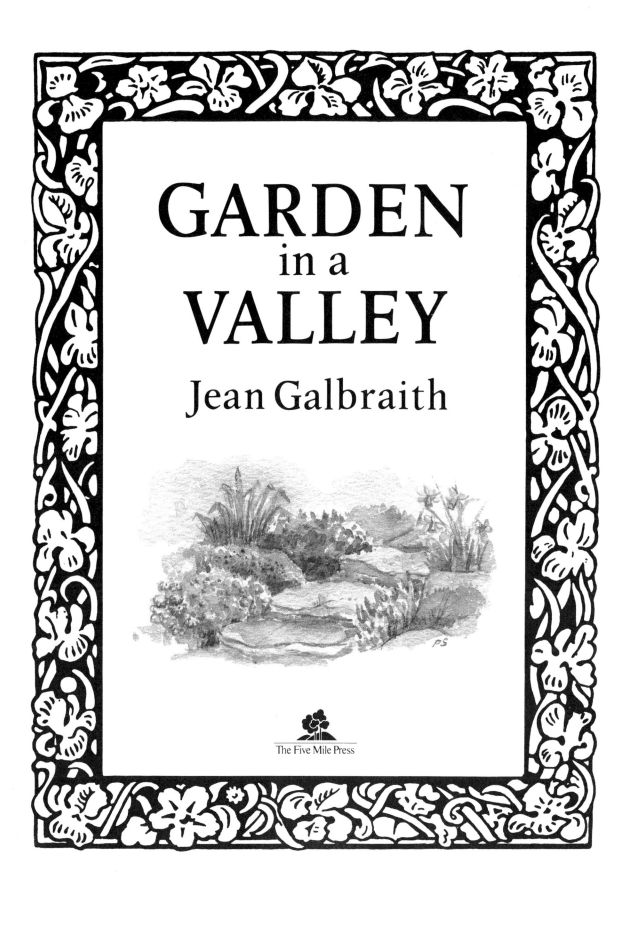

The Five Mile Press

THE FIVE MILE PRESS
20 Liddiard Street
Hawthorn   Victoria   3122   Australia

First Published 1939
This edition published 1985
©Jean Galbraith 1985
Designed by Peter Cuffley
Typeset by Creative Typographics
Printed and bound in Hong Kong by Dai Nippon Printing Co Ltd

National Library of Australia Cataloguing-in-Publication data
Galbraith, Jean.
   Garden in a Valley.
   ISBN 0 86788 075 9.

   1. Galbraith family. 2. Victoria – Genealogy.
   3. Gardening – Victoria. I. Title.
929'.2'0994

Contents

Fern Tree Gully   Nicholas Chevalier

Foreword

At the launching of Peter Cuffley's book *Cottage Gardens in Australia*, three of those present at Harcourt (Helen Vellacott, Peter and I) discussed the possibility of republishing Miss Jean Galbraith's early work describing the building of the garden where she still lives. Our main reason was that suggested in 1970: "*Garden in a Valley* has been out of print for a generation but one continues to hope for another edition of this altogether charming record".[1]

We feel that a new edition of this work would be welcomed by the increasing number of today's readers fascinated by the Australian countryside and its settlement, by the history of its pioneering families and the history of its early gardens with their introduced and native plants.

Jean Galbraith's early schooling was severely curtailed by illness but she speaks with affection of one inspiring teacher, J.W. Elijah, who gave her the run of his library; also, of course, of her home "in which we were all but saturated in poetry and books, and influenced by the Bible — read aloud *every* evening by all of us in succession." But, Jean says, "No one encouraged me to write — I just wrote." In 1926 she began a series of monthly articles in *The Garden Lover*, and this continued without break for fifty years under her pen name "Correa". Some of these early articles make up the chapters of *Garden in a Valley*. Jean's latest book, *A Gardener's Year* to be published by William Collins, reveals her gifts as a writer and as a most acute observer of things worth observing and recording.

Jean and her parents were as much interested in natural history as in their gardens. When she was sixteen, she went (by horse and buggy to Traralgon and by train, four hours to Flinders Street Station) to the Wild Flower Show of the Victorian Field Naturalists Club in Melbourne. There she met H.B. Williamson, a leading naturalist, who became, over his last ten years, her friend and mentor. He identified her specimens, lent her books, "taught me to use the Baron's keys, enough German to puzzle out some botanical papers (I had a smattering of Latin), how to make a herbarium and to write notes on plants." And so Jean became a botanist. She joined the Field Naturalists Club in 1923 and was made a life member in 1959. For over fifty years she contributed papers to the *Victorian Naturalist* and became a friend of all the great field naturalists of the day. She was awarded the Australian Natural History Medallion in 1970. She has played a major role in the naturalist clubs of the Latrobe Valley, where she is widely known and loved.

Jean Galbraith's knowledge of plants and birds is extensive and detailed and she has a real gift for expounding it, both in her writings and in lectures — for years she took part in the CAE Spring Schools in her beloved Alps. She is also the author of two most valuable floras.

[1] Swaby, A.J. and Willis, J.H., *The Award of the Australian Natural History Medallion,* Vic. Naturalist, Vol. 87, No. 10, Oct. 1970.

The first of these *Wildflowers of Victoria* (1950), went through three editions and was widely used when both von Mueller's and Ewart's more conventional floras went out of print. Much later in life she wrote the Collins *Field Guide to the Wildflowers of S.E. Australia*. This covers the flora of the immensely rich and varied region from Adelaide to Brisbane, including Tasmania. Although it does not attempt to replace the major floras of the states represented, it is an invaluable travelling companion for naturalists and botanists. It is a quite remarkable achievement for a naturalist of advanced age living alone near a very small country settlement, 160 kilometres from the major libraries and without a car of her own.

Over the last twelve years, with the wisdom she has gathered about the plants, animals and people of Victoria, she has made her own contribution to nature conservation. This she has done largely through her written submissions on land use to the Land Conservation Council of Victoria. I remember how often the Chairman, the late Mr. S.G.M. Dimmick,

commented on the balance and scholarship of her writings — some of which helped as the basis for recommendations to the State Government. We in Victoria owe much to Jean Galbraith, and it is clear from what follows that we owe a debt to her forebears, settlers and farmers who created gardens to remind them of their homes overseas, but quickly developed a love and understanding of the bush, some of which still survives around the original farms.

In Jean's comfortably shabby and delightful living room at Dunedin, filled with old books, original paintings (several by her friends), pressed plants, sea shells, photographs, personal papers and sets of journals, a side window opens to the bird-table, where there is often a group of satin bower-birds. This room (along with the old garden around it) fully expresses her character — enquiring and tenacious, devout, friendly and tranquil. It expresses her love of life and of living things, so clearly revealed in all her writings.

John Turner

Jean Galbraith's 1985 Foreword

I have never seen the small house at 38 Howe Street, Edinburgh, where Andrew Galbraith, my grandfather, lived. In 1856, when he was about 19, he sailed for Australia in the clipper ship *Lightning*, working his passage as baker's mate. There was a tradition in his family of fine baking. His father prepared banquets for the Queen at Holyrood House. One could prepare decorative banquets more easily than decorative gardens in that street of crowded houses.

Nevertheless, gardening became Andrew's delight in Australia. Though baking was useful in the early years, gardening was his recreation, then and all his life. In Scotland too there were gardeners, when there was opportunity. One afternoon during my only visit to Scotland, Peter, son of the Engineer[1], took us to Culcreugh Castle, home of the Laird, the head of our clan. He was busy with brush and dustpan, collecting the spoil from his visitors' horses. It was good stuff, and would feed his roses.

Soon after Andrew reached Australia, another ship brought John Ross, an Englishman

from Yorkshire, with his children Sarah and James. Andrew probably met Sarah in Beechworth where both lived for some years. In 1859 they were married — Sarah was just 18. They gave the house they built the name of Nithsdale. Perhaps one or both had visited the dales of Nith in Scotland, and been happy there.

Nithsdale in Beechworth was a pleasant house, wide-veranda'd, surrounded by its garden and orchard. It stood below the rocky summit of a low hill, clothed with the native Cypress Pines and dropping suddenly to a gorge with a cascading stream and solid granite bridge. Beyond was the busy goldmining town of Beechworth in the dry hills of north-eastern Victoria. Andrew and Sarah loved the place where they lived with their seven children and Sarah's father and brother. "But," said Andrew in 1877, "we know what life is like in a mining town with sixty hotels; it is no place to bring up five sons and two daughters." Sarah agreed and so did their friend and nearest neighbour, with a wife and young family.

8

Land had been opened for sale in Gippsland and Andrew rode with his friend 300 miles south-westward across Victoria, through Melbourne, and eastward to where the foothills of Mt. Erica in the Baw Baw massif drop in gentle curves towards the Latrobe Valley. From their hilltop they could look southward and see the soft blue of the Strzelecki Ranges which separates the wide Latrobe Valley from the coastal heaths and the sea.

The good alluvial flats of the valley itself had already been allocated, but Andrew and his friend were pleased with their land, not realising that the stringy tussock grasses under the trees made for poor cattle grazing. Fortunately, Andrew's selection included a small area of alluvial land.

They rode home through Melbourne, completing there the necessary formalities of purchase. Andrew had selected two adjoining areas, one each for himself and John Ross, and he returned to Beechworth well satisfied.

It was decided that John Ross, his son James, and his grandson, should leave first, to clear land and build a house, while Andrew wound up his business and sold Nithsdale. A dray was built to fit Big Bob, their largest horse. It was loaded with all necessities for a journey and for clearing and building. This first party of three, with Big Bob, spent three weeks travelling by the coach roads and the barely passable bush tracks, sleeping under the dray at night, baking their bread in a camp oven by the wayside, coming at last to the forested hills which Andrew had named Mt. Hope.

Meanwhile, Andrew and Sarah prepared to travel with the seven children and household goods by coach to Melbourne and by boat to Sale. The partly completed Gippsland railway, built from both ends, had reached Loy Yang, so when the time came they travelled by train from Sale and completed their journey over twelve miles of rough track to the new house, presumably in the dray.

Their new home was in country very different from the rocky hills of Beechworth on the northern side of the Great Divide, with their Longloaf Box, Blakely's Gum, and groves of pointed cypress pines. In the silver-lichened granite outcrops, crevices overflowed with heathmyrtle, nodding Blue-lily and small orchids.

Gippsland's milder climate gave it forest trees, useful when slabs had to be split for building, but making heavy work for John Ross and his two helpers. Dense shrubs and tangles of wiregrass grew on the sheltered slopes, while the gullies were a haven for tree ferns and ground ferns, musk and blanket leaf, and wattle, with lianas of Wonga Vine and Clematis hanging like ropes from the trees. On the drier slopes and ridge the stringybark and Silvertop forests were more open, with silvery grass tussocks and small flowers or patches of lighter scrub under the trees.

It was on one of those ridges that they built the first house — a bark-roofed house with beaten ant-bed floors and slab walls, big enough for eleven people to live in safety for the first years.

Behind them in a blue haze of distance was Mt. Erica. Below them long timbered slopes, often carpeted with maidenhair fern or clothed with scrub wattles, led down to the one precious strip of alluvial soil, always called The Flat. There was a ridge beyond it where they would live later, then gentler slopes that ended in the flood plain of the Latrobe with its swamps and lagoons and thickets of Swamp Paperbark carpeted thickly with moss, and finally the river itself, outlined in soft yellow every spring, against the southern ranges.

There was no time to explore the lowlands then. The house was built and later the roof covered with hardwood shingles, and a row of Monterey Pines planted for a windbreak gave it a name. That first house was The Pines.

There, Andrew and Sarah settled with their family. Sarah must have been very weary — her eighth and last child was born three months later.

Their Beechworth neighbours settled on adjoining land and we heard many stories of their meetings on Saturday nights, alternately at one house or the other, and dancing to the tune of Andrew's violin — he and three of his sons each played several instruments. They stayed overnight, "the girls sleeping on the floor in one room, the boys in another," but they left early next morning to finish their work before eleven o'clock. Then they met at The Pines, where Grandfather John, for long a Baptist local preacher, conducted their simple

Sunday Service. Other families came to the district, with other children ready for school, and John Ross gave a piece of his land for a playground and school. When it opened in 1879, three of Andrew's children, Matthew, Fred and Harry, were amongst the first pupils.

It was on her daily walk to the school that the second daughter Edith killed sixty snakes in one year. She was twelve years old and like her mother, as small and dainty as a Dresden China shepherdess.

In time a new house of sawn timber and iron roof was built, not far from the school — Andrew named it Mt. Hope after the farm. They made a garden and planted trees on the slope above The Flat. The garden was full of roses — pink and white Maman Cochet, Madam Rivers, Saffrano, Cloth of Gold, Souvenir de la Malmaison. There was a rose on each side of the front door and others, now rarely grown, bloomed along the paths, behind the violets. Outside the long veranda, fuchsias hung like crimson embroidery. Grandma's Myrtle grew in a round shrub bed, bordered with white quartz. There is a layered plant of it in my garden now.

Sarah died before I was born — "No wonder," said my mother, "married at eighteen and with so much to do in the next forty years." Sarah's father, my great grandfather, beloved by all the family as she had been, lived and worked on the farm until three weeks before he died at 98 (in 1908). I can just remember him. He must have been very near the end of his life. I was not quite three, and accompanied someone who took him a meal or a cup of tea. As we left his voice followed us down the passage softly. "Thank you, thank you, thank you." he said.

By that time most of his grandsons had married and built houses within ten minutes' walk of Mt. Hope, where a housekeeper cared for Andrew. Only one son, Harry, the Printer, moved to the town. There is no work for a printer on a farm. The daughters moved further away.

The Galbraiths had been friendly with the Ladson family in Beechworth and years later Amy Ladson paid a visit to the Galbraiths in Gippsland. In 1903, Andrew Galbraith's third son Matthew married Amy. They were my parents and they made their home adjoining Mt. Hope, separated only by a small courtyard and the Big Shed. Grapevines grew in the courtyard and I remember them hung with purple grapes. The Big Shed housed the pump, the woodbox, the washing troughs and mangle. A table at one end was so large that it was always used for family gatherings — the last I remember was for my eldest Uncle's Silver Wedding Anniversary. Opposite the Big Shed was the dairy with its cellar for milk and cream and its shelves for apples. Our house was at the east end. At the west, Uncle James Ross had his room, built of slabs from the first house, almost covered with a Wonga Vine, cream and crimson in the springtime. Beyond the gardens of the two houses, north, east and south, stretched the orchard. It was in full bearing when I first remember it. Old apples, Irish Peach, Northern Spy, Blue Pearmain, grew there, with Jargonelle and Winter Cole Pears, oranges, lemons, limes and quinces, Golden Drop plums and cherry plums. West of the orchard, before it dipped down the hill on the south, was Grandfather's vegetable garden, separated from our house by a road of crushed stone from a hill above the flat. The road led to the farm buildings, and was bordered all the way by the shrubbery which Andrew planted with shrubs and hardy bulbs, purple and white irises, blue agapanthus and jonquils. Some of the cypresses that backed the shrubbery still grow there.

Our house was simply named "Home", "because," said mother, "that's what it is." The front veranda was embowered in passion vine, with great crimson flowers, each with its central crest of blue. Below it was mother's garden, with polyanthus, double buttercups and violets, and across the path was father's rose garden, filling all the space between our house and the orchard. Velvet red Dr. Rushpur grew there, and Lord Raglan, lovely single Irish Elegance, and many others with long forgotten names. So often, when father came in from work, he would bring mother one beautiful rose, sharing his pleasure with her.

Andrew died when I was six. When I think of that time I think of violets.

"You must be very good today," mother said, "everyone is sad because grandfather died. Would you like to help me pick violets to put near him?" Soberly, but not really sad, I helped pick the violets. He used to show me his flowers and I loved being with him — but I had not seen him for weeks — a long time when one is six.

When I was eight, we moved from Home to the house where I now live. It was built for Uncle John who moved closer to Melbourne, and to us it seemed spacious, with its four bedrooms — Home had only two. It was about ten minutes walk from Mt. Hope and Home, and it was named "Dunedin" in memory of Edinburgh.

The house was built on a gentle slope of the Latrobe Valley, which still carries some of the surviving trees of the open woodland — Peppermint, Red and Yellow Box, Manna Gum and But-But. It was here, in 1914, that we began to build the Garden in the Valley. It still survives under my care, but today, from the front gate, I can see in the distance the cooling towers and smoke stacks of the great power stations standing near vast open pits of brown coal: our legacy of past forests.

Jean Galbraith, 1985

Acknowledgment

I have always thought it a graceful custom that an author, beginning a book, should acknowledge his indebtedness to those who have helped him. Yet I find myself unable to make any adequate acknowledgment, for my debt is too great.

All that is good in the book or myself has come through the influence of others so that it is impossible to mention all of whom I think with gratitude.

To the proprietors of *The Australian Garden Lover* in which these chapters first appeared, and to Mr. R.E. Boardman the editor of *The Garden Lover* whose faith in my work has alone made the publication of *Garden in a Valley* possible, I here express my thanks.

For the rest I can only say that I am indebted to every one of my friends, to some of them beyond expression or measure.

The world of people and things has given to me with both hands, so that I have been enriched by every day.

I thank you all. It is pleasant to share this happy gardening with you.

Jean Galbraith, 1939

To the above acknowledgments I must add an expression of my gratitude to Professor John Turner and Mr. Peter Cuffley, and to Mrs. Vellacott who started the whole project by lending a book to a friend.

Without any one of them there would have been no new edition of this book.

John Turner and Peter Cuffley have worked untiringly; artists have co-operated with enthusiasm, allowing us to use beautiful pictures without charge, and The Five Mile Press has encouraged us. I am grateful to them all.

Jean Galbraith   1985

Preface

I began to tell the story of this garden nearly four years ago, and spent happy hours living it over again as I wrote. Many other garden makers have written to me, telling of their pleasure in the "Garden in a Valley" though they have never seen it, and I have enjoyed their letters. They remind one that there are happy homes and sunlit gardens everywhere, and since the thoughts of the world have been concentrated more on things of war than things of peace the peaceful things have become sacred.

We need to remind ourselves that there must still be gardens in China and Japan, that even in tortured Spain there are trees and flowers blossoming, and round innumerable homes in Germany and Italy, as in England, flowers are tended and loved by peaceful-hearted folk who want nothing but to live quietly and grow their flowers, and who believe, however wrongly, that if they are forced into war it will be in defence of peace. Yet because there are others who care little for beauty or growth or gentleness the world lives in fear. If we have to face the horror of war let us remember that there are flower-loving hearts all over the world. That knowledge makes war more horrible, but it should also make it impossible for us to hate any nation. When a country is aggressive it is because the harsh natures are its leaders, not because it has no gentleness.

More I could say, since peace is become so precious to us all, but you might think it outside the scope of a garden book.

And now, in the words of four years ago I must tell you about the garden.

It is not a model garden with terraces and wide peaceful lawns; rarely, alas, is it even orderly, for Father, Mother and I are the only gardeners, except when the tall brothers come home for holidays, and the garden is frankly too big for us. Yet we love it as it is and learn much from it, and we think that perhaps others might love it and learn from it too.

It is above all a place of flowers and trees, of roses climbing over arches and covering bush and standard with bloom. There are Delphiniums in it, and tall Foxgloves, gay common Marigolds and Poppies and Daisies; varied foliages, green against grey, grey against brown and red; bulbs that flower in the grass and wattles that smile at each other on winter days, fruit trees and blossom trees and many-clustered vines.

It is always changing and always growing. We grow older with the trees, but youth comes and goes in the garden, having part in it. Tales of love and laughter and sorrow and joy are woven into and enrich it, and the garden enriches them, and they become part of it though the actors come and go.

It is never finished: there is always a dream of something more to do, and we would not have it otherwise. In spite of failures and mistakes and imperfections its airs are sweet, its flowers love to bloom, and we are happy in it.

The foregoing was written in April, 1939, but it is no less true now war has come.   J.G., Nov. 1939.

13

Quiet Study, c.1889   Tom Roberts

The Years of Dream

Where thoughts are singing swallows
And brooks of morning run.
Longfellow

Time passes slowly at the beginning of things; when one is three — and four — and five, years old. And so it seems that we lived for long years in the garden where we were born, the garden we left when I was eight and my brothers four and six.

Years and years of nights, it might have been, we lay in the warm dusk and smelled the fragrance of white jessamine starlike round the open window, and heard the friendly "plomp" of frogs in the pool under the wide black wattle trees. Years and years of mornings we traced the words of "The Lord is my Shepherd" on the long scroll-like picture on the wall, heard the clear note of the grey thrush and hastened out to the verandah with crumbs, saw the garden brimming with roses, the slopes of blossoming orchard on every side, our own gardens, each with its special treasures. Years and years, stretching back to dim forgetfulness, we saw the lamplight across the dusk, and lazily traced the pattern of lilies on the wall, and were sung to sleep, dreamy and warm and as safe as nestling birds.

From the long years of dreams stand out hours of high adventure; hours in the orchard when we gathered apples under the trees, Blue Pearmain and Irish Peach; and the warm sun and all the richness of the hours centred in crisp and mellow apple flavors, and the little green "Christmas Pears" that were crisp and sweet even before they were ripe. It was a memorable hour when we first saw Portulacas, like a many-coloured carpet of glowing petals on the ground. "Grandfather's flowers", we were told, and Grandfather himself, looking down on us with smiling blue eyes, came to show us their beauty. They are like a rainbow across the bright years of dream. In the memory there is a warmth and shining joy, for, at five years old, they seemed the loveliest flowers in all the world. We would no more have gathered them than we would have plucked the petals from a rose.

Very full were the years of dream, and the days of adventure like stars beyond counting, the day when I first saw wattles in bloom, the day when we found the tangle of pink and white monthly roses with yellow horns of honeysuckle all among them, the morning when, passing suddenly, we startled a spinebill from the daphne bush. Yes, time is full and shining and long in the years before seven.

Then we left "Home", the house on the hill,

15

with its rooms full of memories, its garden full of flowers. I do not think we regretted it. It was all delight to move to the larger house in the valley, when we could still look up to the home on the hill. It was a bare white house, with a young oak on one side and an elm on the other, and a row of pines for a windbreak on the west.

Through all the years that come after seven the voice of the pines forms an undertone, and sunsets are framed by them. Many joys were in those years: golden skies patterned by the Sunset Trees which crowned a western hill, the tree-arched road past the gate leading from sunrise to sunset, its air sweet with song. Perhaps the years from seven to seventeen, and even farther, are not less years of dream.

There was little garden round the valley home, a border in the empty yard, a narrow, carefully tended bed that ran down the west side of the house, from the north corner, sixty yards southward to the front gate, on the east side one rose, a Frau Karl Druschki, to which summer brought white flocks of bloom. Between the long west border and the pines was the wilderness, a damp patch of rushes and scrub, but wonderland to us, with its red shelf fungi, its one peppermint with quaint fruits, and, beyond the rushes, a fragrant brown carpet of needles, always dry, where we built tepees with brushwood, and, playing "Dog Crusoe", buried each other with needles instead of leaves.

In front of the house, and eastward, was an orchard of stunted trees, with grass and weeds under them, and many gaps where winter wet and summer heat had taken toll, for there was no water supply then, and summer dealt hardly with us, and in winter the poor grey soil became sucking mud, as in summer it had been lumpy cement.

It was little wonder that there could be no garden made during those early years, yet we three, my brothers and I, had our gardens from the first. The long border above the yard was divided into three beds, each carefully edged with bricks, with a daisy border.

It was when we made the new garden that we were given our first packets of Children's Garden Seeds — fat sixpenny packets full of mixed seeds of hardy flowers. What flowers we grew from them! Poppies of every colour, linarias, clarkias, larkspurs (white and blue), lupins pushing up like great beans and unfolding lovely fingerlike leaves above everything but the hollyhocks. How carefully we chose our seed boxes, the widest we could find, and set them by the sunny eastern wall. How eagerly we collected broken crocks to make a layer under the soil, and how conscientiously we mixed leafmould and sand, sifted through flywire, and filled the boxes, and watered them and left them (how impatiently!) till the next day, before scattering the seed.

We would open the packets the same night, and tip the contents on to a plate, as a prelude to exciting discoveries. We would pick out the big ones: lupin, nasturtiums, sweet peas, which we knew, and peer at the others with a magnifying glass. "Pansy seed!" we would proclaim joyfully, picking out shiny golden-brown ovals! "Stocks!" pouncing on pale discs; "Wallflowers!" finding bright brown ones.

There were others which mother knew, though we could not recognise them: Scabious, with a bristly star on top of its little column; Cornflower, with a tuft of hair in its smooth quill; dust-like sand, that was poppy seed, and others, brown, strawcoloured, black, which none of us knew.

Daily, after we planted them, lightly covered, they were watched, covered from rain, sprinkled with luke-warm water from a brush when the surface dried. A wet hairbrush, shaken lightly over them, made a softer rain than any watering-can.

There was new excitement when the first seedlings appeared. We learned to know the cotyledons of many. The clearly veined discs of hollyhocks came first, then round blue-green stocks and tiny dinted clarkias. Others we did not know till the second leaves came; now and then we had to wait for flowers.

We watched them impatiently, counting the leaves. "When there are six pairs of leaves you may plant them in the garden," we were told, and in preparation for that great day the gardens were dug and raked. Until we learned them for ourselves, Father and Mother would point out the tallest kinds, hollyhocks, lupins, cornflowers, and we would plant them carefully at the back of the bed, each with its ring of lime "to keep the slugs away". The seedlings were planted very close together — too close —"But then some always die," we said comfortably, and so they did, in spite of the lime, and some were disturbed and wilted after too vigorous weeding or raking, yet when blossom time came the gardens were full.

Clear among shining memories is the flowering of the mimulus. Among all the packets there was but one mimulus, a soft luxuriant plant, recognised as a stranger from the first. "Monkey Musk," said Mother delightedly, when it had grown into a sturdy plant, and she told us of spotted bells, crimson and gold. Then one morning we found, in place of the folded bud, a flower as big as a foxglove bell, orange, crimson blotched. It was hard to go into breakfast and leave it looking out above the opening pansies.

Then that very week baby brother arrived, and Mother had no time for gardening till long afterwards. Even her little border of violets and primroses and stocks under the diningroom window was left to itself for a while, and Father, too, was busy in those days. So we gardened alone, lovingly, if irregularly, and arranged vases full of our flowers for the table, sure of warm and discerning admiration from the two who had made us gardeners.

The years were still years of dream, though school had come into our lives, stealing so many glorious hours. School, for me, meant but a short walk from home, so I could watch the garden grow, but for my brothers, growing up and preparing for the University, it meant, when State School days were over, long absences in the city. Meanwhile, the wilderness became a paddock with a washaway like a little gully through it, and one blackwood, gracious with cream bloom against the pines. And between the house and the gate was a long path through the grass tussocks and stunted fruit trees.

In time a fence separated the "garden" (three fruit trees, a path, and a long stretch of weeds) from the orchard, where trees were more numerous and weeds and docks grew wild. Then, because it was too rough to dig, the ground was ploughed, and two more long paths, converging at the gate, marked through it, two long drains following its southern slope, dug and covered — then the ground lay fallow until school holidays brought the two elder brothers home from school. Their gardens then had little care, but they spent many hours trenching the waste that was to be the new garden, burying loads of rubbish, breaking the cold subsoil, but looking at it now, at its growth, luxuriant even at mid-winter, its brown soil crumbling and workable in July, surely the labourers think their task was worth both labour and weariness.

Thus the garden began. I have shown it to you, an untrained child garden almost without promise, but now I look down that long path, where the ploughing used to be, through arch after arch of roses. In spring they make it a rainbow path with fallen petals. Primroses and Polyanthus, white and blue and crimson, purple and tawny and gold, border it thickly, clustering in their crinkled leaves, while above them ranunculus look up to the roses and all the mixture of bright flowers that makes the spring air glow. The orchard beyond is full of fruitful trees, the wilderness has become the woodland. But that is today; only the foundations of these were laid in those last bright years of dream. We have water in summer now, and flowers all the year, so that we can look at the beauty the path divides and say, marvelling: "Can it be ours!"

Fern gully, Gippsland

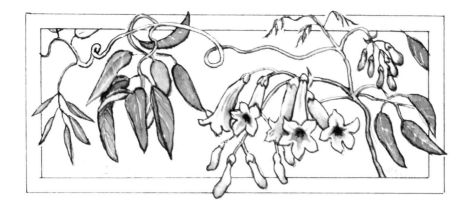

Building a Bush House

In a pixie wood where the sunshine's gold
Hid in the moss, and instead of flowers
Were toadstools yellow and toadstools red
And a birds nest hung by the path ahead.

J.G.

The wilderness where we had built wigwams and climbed trees was no ideal patch of bush which we could preserve and delight in. It was rather starved and scrubby, and there was marshy ground in the centre, hidden by green swathes of rushes. We were forbidden to go through them, and had to skirt the edge to reach our playground under the pines.

"Remember snakes," Mother would call after us as we went there to play, and we did remember, for we had a wholesome fear of them. We rarely saw one, but I remember how, one hot afternoon when Father and Mother were away, we found a young one on the path and killed it valiantly with the axe.

Later the wilderness was drained and cleared of all but one young blackwood tree. Bob came from a home far back in the hills to do the work. He was a big boy, quiet and humorous and kind, who later went reluctantly, but with a resigned sigh, to the war, and the war sent him home — to live for a year or two. He was very patient with us as we stood round while he worked, watching him sink the straight sides of the drain and chattering meanwhile.

From the bush paddock across the road he brought young saplings, smelling of gum, and filled the drain with them, piling the clayey soil on top. This hastened the drying of the wilderness which the pines were doing more effectively every year, and for the next few years the cleared ground was used as a fowl yard. It grew more attractive each year, and by the time the fowls were excluded from it there was quite a thicket of young blackwoods round the shapely parent trees; the drain had fallen in, forming an open gulley, and the ground which was later to become the Woodland was mantled with flowering grasses.

When the Yorkshire Fog Grass spread its plumes of pink and brown and grey we walked waist deep in it, yet with an eye on the ground for snakes, and gathered bunches of it mixed with Blown Grass, which from a tight little spire opens suddenly into a crown of thread-like stems, as light as gossamer.

Each month brought its sign to the grasses. November brought golden hosts of Dandelions, then their seed ripened into grey "clocks" in December, and blew away, leaving empty heads. Almost before they were sere came the deep autumnal rains and springing green, the slow growth of winter, and then it was spring again.

19

So the time passed, the elder brothers went away to school, baby brother was a baby no longer; he too was at school, and the garden grew, as I have told you, from a child garden to beautiful luxuriance, though its trees were still young.

Work went hand in hand with happiness; we were ever making new plans, the wildflower border whose tale is told elsewhere was being made, and we spoke of a bush house "some-day". I do not remember now what made us definitely decide to build it, but I remember that one day Father and Mother and I stood below the north fence of the Wilderness, where the drain had washed out deepest, talking of it.

"If we make it here," said Father, "we have part of one wall already," for the fence there was three foot palings.

"If we make it here," said I, seeing visions of what might be, "we have the gully and need only the ferns."

So we spent that evening drawing plans. We decided that the bush house was to be fifteen feet by twenty, with walls six feet high and a pointed roof.

"We want room for tree-ferns, big tree-ferns," we said, so the apex of the roof was to be six feet higher than the walls, fourteen feet higher than the bed of the gully.

Fortunately there is usually spare timber on a farm. It was all gathered up and any time that Father could take from his work was spent in building the framework of the bush house.

"And now," he said, "we will wait for the holidays."

With the holidays the boys came home, and a party of friends, several of them schoolboys, came to camp. They helped us cart loads of green tea-tree and wire it like thatch over the frame of the bush house. They made a game of the work, which occupied them for two burning January days, while Mother and I saw to it that the supply of raisin scones and blackberry vinegar was equal to the demand.

I still wonder whether it was really a game to them, or whether they thought ungrateful thoughts about the holiday entertainment we had planned for them. It was hot and some of the tea-tree was prickly. Yet there must have been some pleasure in it. Most of the green

loads they brought were fragrant paper-bark limbs, very dark and cool, and when it was finished the big oblong, with its green walls and pointed roof, was like a new kind of Wendy House.

It was too hot and dry for fern planting at that time, so for three months we watched the green fade to grey and brown and the narrow leaves fall upon the empty ground.

While we waited we prepared for the ferns. In the evenings Father wove wire baskets for them, and I spent happy hours in the tea-tree paddock gathering moss to line the baskets with. It was bright green moss, so thick that one sometimes sank more than ankle deep into it. There are many acres in the tea-tree paddock, and not a few of them were carpeted like this. They were dotted with brown and yellow fungi, columned by tea-tree stems, and the edges were wreathed with crimson trails of blackberry, and sweet briar grew there with its scarlet fruits. As children we often went there gathering moss, and in spite of the pleasure of slipping one's hand underneath and peeling off a cool damp carpet of it, we always felt regretful as we took it away. I do not think we ever did it without covering the bare spot with branches "to mend it", and putting back a few little tufts to grow again.

The baskets were lined and filled with leaf mould from under the trees, and all the ferns we had in pots were planted in them. The long fronds of Boston Fern hung like a waterfall from one; several were lacy with maidenhair; in three we planted plectranthus with its purple backed leaves.

When the baskets were finished it was autumn, and cool enough for other work. On one joyful day Father brought home a load of stones, green stained with lichen, and built up the sides of the gully, leaving pockets where ferns could nestle. Then he dug the ground that sloped up to the walls on each side, terracing it a little.

We stood at the doorway and looked at the empty space as an artist might at a bare canvas when paints stood ready to his hand. From the house, where they had stood against a shelter-ed wall, we took down hardy begonias and shade loving fuchsias in their pots, and the baskets of ferns were all suspended. Then we waited. The ground was still too dry for planting.

But one cool April day it rained steadily, soaking the gully banks.

"If it's fine tomorrow," said Father, on the second wet day, "we will go and get ferns."

We told each other before we left that we would take only little plants, and whence they could not be missed. As I have never heard of anyone else who visited the steep mountain gulley, since burned, where we gathered them, it would not have mattered if we had taken large ones.[1]

What a day it was! The clear air was sunlit and cool and the softness of autumn growth was on the hills. We drove up the long road and then twisted in and out among trees along a ridge till it was too rough to drive farther. There we left the jinker and rode the two horses downhill until Midge, who carried me, stopped, afraid to go on, though Father's big bay with the wise kind eyes, would have carried him to the hill's foot. We tied the two horses on the most level spot we could find, and went down into a world of ferns, slipping more often than walking at the last, till we stood beside a stream that only whispered, so softly it flowed. About us were ferns more beautiful than our happiest dreams of those that were to grow in the bush house gully.

The trunks of mountain grey gums rose through them, columnar and pale, to some invisible height above the musk and ferns where we knew there were smooth boughs and clouds of leaves. On every side were tree ferns, their trunks clothed with translucent Filmy Ferns with a drop of water trembling on the tip of every frond. There were mosses so frail that one hardly dared breathe on them, covering logs and rocks; the chocolate soil was clustered over with ferns, and yellow robins slipped through them with a gleam of primrose breasts. Here was strap fern, with its pink young fronds, here a baby waterfall; a lyre bird's nest; blanket-leaf spreading its crown of stars against the white trunks of the gums. We unpacked our lunch beside the little stream and while we were eating the robins flew near us, taking crumbs we dropped for them, flying

even between us, so that we felt the movement of their wings. How could we take ferns from such a wonderland! Yet we took them, and the gully was not visibly poorer.

We dug up one here and one there, wrapping them in paper and packing them in bags, then with a last look at the fern-kissed stream, a last breath of the fragrance of moss and frond and fallen leaves, we began to climb back to where the horses, Tom and Midge, waited patiently on the hillside. I carried the spade, I remember, and the lunch case and a bag of ferns, so no doubt Father had at least twice as much. But we took different routes and I do not remember his journey, though I shall not forget mine. I would fix my eyes on a log some distance ahead and think firmly, "*I won't* sit down till I reach that," and when it seemed impossible to go a step farther I would sink on it limply, taking out the bottle of milk we had not used and drinking thankfully. I do not like milk, but that day it was delicious.

It was good to reach Midge at last, inexperienced rider though I was, and better still to sit in the jinker with the ferns at our feet, and drive homeward along the white hill road. We went happily to bed that night and woke to adventure — the planting.

The soil was still cool and damp and our rocky crevices ready for their ferns. We planted strap fern in one, water ferns in others, laid a piece of dead treefern trunk grown over with kangaroo fern along one edge, set Austral Elderberry here, lomatia there. The bush house planting was really begun.

Treasures were added from time to time, but slowly. There were, as with the wildflowers, gifts, purchases, exchanges, and the special addition of that year was a bird's nest fern, then six inches, but now several feet, in diameter. Father found it in that place of glad discoveries, the "Flowering" columns of the newspaper, where now and again lovely things are advertised for sale for a few pence each. It is a place full of pitfalls, but one soon learns which nurserymen may be trusted. Indeed, it is rarely nurserymen from whom the disappointments come, but from dealers re-selling plants which they have bought.

[1] With our 1980s population and commercialisation it would be disastrous to remove plants as we did 50 years ago. It is now illegal to do so.

GARDEN IN A VALLEY

Our ferns established themselves and made new fronds during winter and spring. Then came the first summer. There were strong west winds that swept under the pines and through the tea-tree walls; there were hot, dry days when our taps were waterless and all the water used had to be pumped by hand from a limited supply. By the end of the summer the bush house was drooping and weary. Many ferns had died, and when we thought of their cool gully home we feel that we were vandals. We did not know then that a bushfire had swept it into one sheet of flame.

That autumn too was unusually dry. Even ferns that had survived the summer looked desolate. And then, in April, came the news that two friends were coming to see our garden. They were both garden lovers, well-known through their writings, whose precepts had guided many, and had helped us for years.

I looked at the bush house in dismay. Must we show them *that?* We were filled with shame. It happened that the two younger brothers were at home just then, and co-operated warmly in my hastily made plans. We could not make much of the place, but it could be improved. It was emptied, so far as could be, and rearranged. Dead ferns were taken out, and the boys made a rapid journey with spades and sugar bags to the nearest fern gulley (already disappearing beneath the axe and plough of the owner). They brought back a supply of hardy ferns, shield fern and rasp fern and maidenhair. They were planted hastily, watered well, and next day, though not very full and quite without rarities, the fern house

did not wholly belie its name. We ran down to peep at it before breakfast, and smiled at each other with satisfaction.

The visitors praised generously, and entered into all our triumphs, able to see not only what was, but also what would be, and even what was meant to be.

We went out with them into the southern hills, and spent a memorable day among the myrtle-beech and sassafras and ferns of the Strzlecki Ranges, thirty miles away. There, from a roadside cutting hung with ferns, one of our visitors dug two tree ferns, an inch or so high, with his pocket-knife, and laid them in my hand.

"We will save two at least," he said, knowing that the place was too exposed for them.

They are growing in the bush house now, tree ferns with trunks two feet high and fronds sweeping across the doorway.

There was never another summer that took toll like that first one. We have learned through experience what we should have known when the bush house was built. It is not heat, or even dryness, but wind that kills ferns most quickly. Inside the bush house the six foot walls on the west and south, whence come nearly all our winds, were boarded closely, and though the bush house is still not full, and one far corner has become a bed for rooting cuttings in, the whole has some likeness to a fern gully again.

"Never plant creepers in a bush house," says every book on the subject, and we agree that the rule is good, yet we do not observe it. On the first day of gathering among the hills we brought home Wonga Vine and clematis and

The bush house

22

Stooks and children, "Dunedin", c.1918

planted them on either side of the door. Now the walls and roof are covered with green. The Wonga Vine tosses handfuls of crimson throated bells from every spray in early spring. Clematis follows with starry blossom and silken seed which the summer feathers into a cloud of silver grey. By the door the wild passionflower of East Gippsland uncurls its red and yellow flowers and hangs its round green fruits, and till a few years ago there were purple curtains of Hardenbergia on the west, "Sarsaparilla", which from childhood we have counted among September's chief joys. We have never kept one growing in this garden for more than three years, though for many more years than that one made a glory in the garden on the hill.

We know that we should not grow creepers on the bush house, but, whatever failings there are inside it, its exterior justifies its existence, so we would not change it.

An Elderberry Panax, straight and slender, stands beside the door, and drops its opal berries near the close of the year, and young panax suckers spread strong, beautiful leaves inside. Austral Mulberry and Golden Tip grow near the eastern wall, their feet in a wave of Cockspur Flower. The Golden Tip is like laburnum in spring, and at new year the mulberry hides yellow astringent fruits among its shining leaves. There is a peach tree by the north wall, pressing its rosy boughs against the creepers, and later making a feast of small fruits for a family of possums whose nest is in the Woodland.

Yet in spite of all these, in spite of the wattles behind and scented paperbark below, it is light enough in the bush house for the ferns still living there to thrive.

Much has happened during its growth. The garden has grown side by side with it, and we have grown also. Baby Brother is not even a schoolboy now. We call him the Student, and the elder brothers are not even students, except in their leisure. They have become the Teacher and the Engineer. But I am still Correa, the gardener, and here still are Father and Mother, making it home for us all.

23

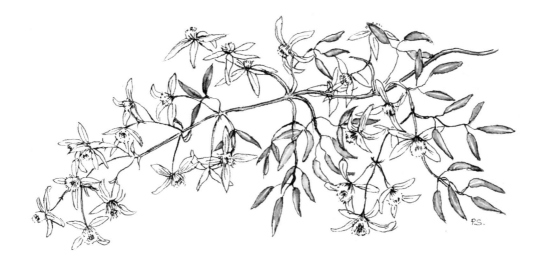

Wildflowers

The arborets and flowers which of itself
this land pours forth profuse.

Dante

Ever since we came to live in the valley we have tried to grow wildflowers. Even into our first gardens, among all the revelry of the poppies and linarias, we used to move Blue Stars and Nodding Greenhoods — and they always died.

At the cost of many little lives we bought our experience, and it is still rather a puzzle why the plants which we moved with such care never grew, while now even cuttings will thrive for us.

We did learn a few things by precept, and Mr. Pescott's "Native Flowers of Victoria" was our chief and well-loved guide. We learned to move always small plants, with their roots undisturbed, to give them well-drained soil, to establish them in pots before putting them out in the open garden, to shade and mulch them in summer.

Thus gradually the store of wildflowers thriving in pots, or, more often, in jam tins, increased, for we never saw a new or beautiful wildflower, or fern or tree without searching through the surrounding bracken (there is bracken everywhere on our hills) for a seedling small enough to transplant. From this store of plants, clamouring for more room, grew the plan for the wildflower border.

There were three long paths through the garden, the east path, the west path, the middle path, and between the east path and the orchard was a long narrow bed. This, we decreed, should become the wildflower border. So the soil was trenched, though not manured except with vegetable refuse, and left to settle, and in April, after the deep soaking rains, but before the autumn warmth had gone from the soil, the planting began.

We used in those days to establish most of our plants in jam tins, which, when their occupants were ready for transplanting, were cut down with a tin-opener and removed without disturbing root or soil. But first a hole was dug, a little deeper and wider than the pot (we called them "pots" by courtesy), a stake set firmly in it, and light sandy soil mixed with the heavy loam that we had removed. Then, as carefully as if a breath would spoil it, the plant was taken from its pot, pressed into the hole, but not pressed so hard that the soil broke from the roots, and watered, even though the garden was wet, before the hole was filled with the sandy mixture packed tightly round the new plant.

"The roots are like little children," said

Happy bush children, c.1908

Mother, "they don't want hard food at first."

In the first planting were Queensland Silver Wattle, Hazel Pomaderris, Hill Banksia (which delighted us next year with its "maize-cob" flowers), Silky Hakea, Rosemary Grevillea, Red Correa, bush-pea. They were well spaced down the long border with small plants — heath, beard-heath, pink bell, parrot-pea — usually in little clusters of several of the same kind, between them. We were full of high hope. We pictured the border, in a few years, as a rainbow — and it is a rainbow, though not just such a one as we planned, for some plants, taking kindly to the soil, spread luxuriantly, others, less adaptable, were dwarfed, or died, and new ones took their place. One needs to know a plant better than we knew them then, better than we know most of them now, before one can guess with certainty its reaction to a new soil. Can we even guess how it would affect ourselves if we were lifted from familiar homes and set among strangers, and told to be happy in new ways!

The bed widened at the far end of our wildflower border, cutting diagonally across a corner near the gate. There, overlooking the road, we planted an Early Black Wattle (Queen Wattle we call it more often), which had come from a nursery, a weakling ten inches high. Mother took it for her care, as she took all "special" or feeble plants, planted it, staked with a stout stake, ambitiously tall, in a kerosene tin filled with leaf mould and sand. On stormy nights it was sheltered, on frosty nights during the first winter it was brought indoors, and during the summer, though it was watered enough to prevent any check of growth, it was not so pampered that it would be too soft to stand an outdoor position later.

Mother had watched over it for nearly two years when we planted it — it was over three feet high, with tough ridged stems and leaves like a shadowy dark veil.

We all gathered for the planting; Father cut the tin right to the base in two places, and opened but did not remove it; we knew it would rust away in the ground, and the hole was quite big enough to contain it. Were we planting it now we might take less care, and it would probably grow, but we have never regretted the time bestowed on it. Was not the care itself delight! And without it perhaps the tree had not been quite so fair. Not one leaf drooped. From year to year the tree increased in beauty and stature, and now it is forty feet high, a pyramid of whispering gold, which none who has seen dare try to describe. Yearly we look up and give thanks for it; yearly its lovers come to visit it.

"We just came across to see the wattle tree," say neighbours from the scattered homes of our little township, pausing by the garden gate on Sunday afternoon, and we join

them, glad of some excuse to look at it again, to touch with light fingers its abundant gold. In August it dominates the garden like a violin that soars while its accompaniment flows softly, ministering to its beauty but never disputing its supremacy.

By October it has taken its place in the full harmony of trees — its gold is shed — its rich green blends with the quieter tones of Box and Peppermint on the road beyond it.

Not all our first plantings have grown on triumphantly like this. The Hakea, after delighting us for years with creamy bloom and dark foliage, fell during an autumn storm, when the ground was soft after a week of rain, and a sharp wind caught its water-laden branches. We straightened it, firmed the soil

Out collecting, c.1920

round it, tied it to a post, but it withered from that day. The needles turned brown, a lovely color, like bright pine needles, and its innumerable fruits opened like butterflies as the branches dried. Each brown, roughly pear-shaped woody fruit, split down the centre, and on one of the flat surfaces lay a winged black seed. The seed itself rested in a small hole which fitted it as closely as a sheath its bud, and on the opposite half was another hole which corresponded exactly to the raised half of the seed, while a mark on the flat surface showed the outline of a paper-like wing. All this was revealed when our silky hakea died. Hundreds of rough brown fruits "just like snails!" exclaimed a visitor, opened their dark wings, and as the opened wings of a butterfly reveal unsuspected colors so did these. Half of each, from base to tip, was red; the other half was white, matching the outline of the black seed wing, which had fluttered down with its charge as the fruit opened. So our dead hakea was covered with red and white butterflies till we took it away to crackle on a bonfire. It was too prickly for any other means of disposal. But it did not end there. Path and border alike were strewn with seeds, and on path and border that spring appeared a forest of young hakeas, from which we selected one, the strongest, which is blooming now where its parent fell.

Others were planted outside the orchard fence, where a few survive. "So beautifully thorny," said someone inhospitably, but the children who wriggle through waving grass to the trees in apple time, eager for adventure though they have abundant fruit at home, do not find the little hakea discouraging. What are thorns but a new difficulty to triumph over!

Some of that first wildflower planting we lost because we had not mulched the soil around them. They were then too small to shade each other, and the heat of the summer, beating on the soil near the roots, killed many. Had we known it, half as much water (though we could give them little) and twice as much root protection might have saved their lives.

One or two grew happily for a year, then died because they had not been firmly staked. A heavy wind, which can sway them back and forth in the ground is fatal to many wildflowers.

But most of our plantings grew, and most are still beautiful. The Clematis, planted on the fence wreathed it with stars, and flinging out long tendrils caught the pear tree and climbed up joyously, until, in a year or two, it dropped blossomy sprays from the high boughs, and flung a white veil over the tree top when its own cupped blooms were shed.

Heaths blossomed and dropped their seed; the Nodding Blue-lily became an azure cloud, a new generation grew up under the Prickly Bush-pea, red and green correas grew together, until we had to cut their spreading branches where they blocked the path.

Dozens of plants have been added since the border was made. Bauera, thryptomene, Leafless Bitter-pea, with its red-brown flowers, came from the Grampians, cassia from the Mallee, fringe-myrtle from the hills of north-eastern Victoria. By many ways our plants have come. Rough Parrot-pea, red-flowered, which the sender well described as a "little gem," was an exchange. Long-leaf Waxflower came from a nursery, and now plants of two generations, cuttings from it, grow in other parts of the garden.

For a long time we could not grow cuttings of plants like these. Again and again Father planted them. The nursery was his province, and there he worked with cuttings and seedlings, working, experimenting, where we would have given up long before and been content with easier plants. But success comes often now. We take pieces at all seasons, planting them in sandy soil in a pot covered with glass, for some will grow at one season, some at another. Sometimes we plant hardwood cuttings, but usually the ones that grow are the soft-growing tips, a few inches long, which push out as the flowers fall.

There is no flower in the garden that has not its remembered history. This is from a seed, that from a plant lifted during a bush walk, another came from a much longer journey. Some are cuttings, some gifts, some exchanges. A few are nursery-grown plants, and these too, have their histories — this one is a birthday gift, that a surprise present brought home after a Melbourne holiday.

The two Fairy Waxflowers, than which we have no lovelier plant, were cuttings from a bunch of flowers bought at a barrow in the city, where their starry flowers and rose-pink buds were as fresh and delicate as dew among the heavy blooms of red Carnations and bunched Snapdragons which made such a gallant show.

Father planted dozens of cuttings of these, and Mother and I had each a few, which were moved daily to catch the sun[1], but of all these, two alone survived, growing in sand with a cleaned negative to cover them. When they were an inch high, still in the sand, they bloomed, and they are flowering still.

We no longer use tins for our wildflowers. When pots, which can be used over and over again, cost less than a penny each, there is little reason against getting them, and it is easier to slip a plant out of a pot than to cut it out of a tin.

There is no season now when there is not bloom in the wildflower border. We can plant nothing more there, for it is already full, and, despite the November cutting back, which for the time being carpets the path with branches and fragrant leaves, it threatens to overflow both path and fence. It is never cultivated, though it is weeded once or twice a year, but the weeding can be done in an hour, for the plants grow so closely that there is not much room for other growth.

At the end of the spring, before the first hot days, it is mulched thickly with half-decayed oak leaves saved from the past autumn, and, so protected, summer does it little harm. An empty tank in a sheltered corner takes each day's fallen leaves, rustling and brown and fragrant, piled up above the rim, till one of us climbs up on the brown cone and treads it flat, sinking at first on the crisp and yielding layers. Later we pour water on them to hasten their decay, so that when they are spread on the garden, cool and deep, they will not blow away, but mix with the soil and feed and shelter the hungry roots.

How the garden has grown into our lives! Its treasures are one with our memories, every gift speaks of the giver, every wildling of the day we gathered it. Every plant grown from a cutting recalls the triumph with which we realised another success (for our losses in cuttings are still many, our successes always sweet).

In intrinsic beauty the garden is not behind the bright exotic flowers. In October, it glows with bloom, with gold of wattle and bush-pea, with rosy purple, lilac and mauve, of mint-bushes, red-brown parrot-peas, the starry gold and primrose of pomaderris, blue of speedwell and blue-lily, red and gold grevilleas, starry fringe-myrtle, waxflower like daphne. All these blossom together, and in them is a contented humming of bees, and the tinkling of the spine-bill's little silver bell; with fragrance at once aromatic and warm and sweet. Across the path trees and flowers from other lands smile at them, comrades all in the beauty of the east path, which is now an aisle of bloom and green.

[1] We know now that cuttings do best in shade.

Front path, "Dunedin", 1984 (Photo by Peter Cuffley)

Roses

What is a nation?   It may be here,
Just the same   It may be there;
Old garden with   We grow the same roses
A different name.   Everywhere.

Reginald Arkell

While the east path was becoming the wild-flower path, the long centre path became our Via Rosarius, the Way of the Roses. Roses were the first plants set by it after it was made. But that was not the beginning of our rose growing, which goes back to the garden on the hill. It seems to divide into two periods. During the first we grew a few roses and loved them, knowing little of what other growers were doing. During the second we found ourselves, by means of books and magazines and catalogues, and especially through the National Rose Society's *Rose Annual,* members of a whole family of rose lovers, all ready to exchange experiences, to help each other in difficulty and enjoy each other's triumphs. We were a very unimportant part of the family, rose lovers who could never deserve the dignified title of rosarians, yet we enjoyed the warmth of the friendly intercourse, and the roses benefited from our increased knowledge.

Roses seem to have more individuality than other flowers. One speaks of them by name and they move through the story of the garden as men and women through the larger world. They seem to have more likes and dislikes, more variety of character, than other flowers,

yet that may seem so to us only because we have lived with them so long and known them so well.

They are like human beings, not one of them without its beauty of hidden structure, however varied the outer form may be, and not one without some variety in the more delicate gifts of scent and colour. Each one is interesting, yet how much difference there is between the poor little purplish clusters and mildewed foliage of Veilchenblau and an unfolding Madame Butterfly or a Sunny South in full bloom. How environment affects them, too. A wrong position rarely kills, but it checks most roses woefully. See Talisman in heavy well-worked soil, where a royal flood of morning sunshine bathes it. It is a miracle, a big bush full of eager growth, with every colour of sunset in its flowers, there orange and vermilion, here pink and apricot and cream. But look at Talisman again, with tall growth crowding round it and its roots clogged with wet grey soil. The poor little twigs can hardly hold up their flowers, yet they do flower, bearing pale one-sided, yet often sunset coloured, blooms among leaves that are spotted and yellow, falling too soon beneath the curse of black

31

spot. There are some gallant roses which would have survived even this environment, have triumphed over it and made their surroundings beautiful, but they are few, and so much should not be asked of them. Sunny South is one of these dauntless ones.

Father was always our rose grower. His roses filled most of the garden on the hill, and we knew their names as though they had been the names of playmates. Big Lord Raglin grew near the path where his thorns would tear our pinafores unless we walked warily. I used to think of him as very important gentleman in red robes, a friend of the Queen perhaps, and I looked with great respect but little affection at his gigantic blooms, so different from the dainty little Madame Rivers, with her shell pink face and lips always ready to kiss, only one would not kiss them really, for they looked as if even the gentle little breath of two years old might hurt them.

Irish Elegance grew in a corner. She was a fairy, a radiant miracle, coming and going quickly. There was Cecile Brunner, too, the fairy rose, but more like a rosy little baby really, just the right size for us, so we were allowed to pick the flowers, "but carefully, like this," Mother would show us, "so you don't hurt the bush."

Biggest of all, Frau Karl Druschki, dominated the garden. We used to admire its white blooms, yet there was no animation or friendliness in them till Father held a Dr. Rushplur beside one; Dr. Rushplur, like crimson plush, with petals exquisitely folded. The white rose seemed to gain meaning and personality then.

"Grandfather's garden" was close to ours. Only the big camellia and a lauristinus, and a giant aloe with blue-green leaves edged with butter yellow, divided the two. In Grandfather's garden were roses older than even ours, the Castor Oil rose, smelling unpleasantly, but beautifully yellow like a little sun, moss roses, La France, Souvenir de la Malmaison whose fat pink buds we loved; Saffrano with its apricot flowers, lovely when half open; Bessie Brown, who was rather stodgy, we thought, till one day a bud opened with a glistening heart like watermelon flesh and curled more delicately than a shell. Cloth of Gold was there too, and Pink Maman Cochet — "Isn't he a fine

gentleman, always courteous and honourable!" said Grandfather one day, holding a Maman Cochet against a half open La France. He smiled at his own words: "La France isn't a fine gentleman," he said, "he is an honest working man, just as brave and as good as Maman Cochet, but different," and he looked down at me, his "little companion," with kind blue eyes that smiled, "they are all our friends, aren't they, little maid?"

Most of the beloved roses of those days would be disappointing if compared with roses grown now, but the garden in the valley has never given us Maman Cochets quite like the "fine gentlemen" of Grandfather's garden. There were pink and white Maman Cochets in the valley garden when we came to it, but no other roses, except Frau Karl Druschki on the east wall. Then soon after the long path, now our "Way of Roses" was made, as the first step towards a garden, Father dug circles out of the grass and weeds and planted rooted rose cuttings there. Water was scarce; weeds were many, and few of the roses survived. They struggled for a long time, then gave in, all but three or four, of which two only remain, Cecile Brunner and Frau Karl Druschki. Others like Devoniensis and Saffrano, though they lived, were moved to another and less conspicuous place. They are gentle people and their present green home by the west fence suits them better than the bright petalled company of the Via Rosarius.

It was not until most of the roses had died that anything more could be done to the garden. It was then that it was ploughed, and the side paths made, and we began to have hope that the waste might yet become a place of flowers.

Voting for the first "Argus" Rose Plebiscite was just beginning at the time. We read the lists every day, following their progress eagerly, but realised with some dismay that most of the names were quite strange to us. We — rose lovers, who had been familiar (perhaps just a little proudly familiar) with long names like Devoniensis ever since we had been able to speak — knew by sight only one rose amongst the final twelve. We began to hunger to know more.

Then, the next Christmas, someone gave

Father *The Australasian Rose Book*, by R.G. Elliott. That was the match that started the ready flame. That year, for the first time since we came to the valley, it was possible to give a considerable amount of time to the garden. During the winter also, the friend who gave us the Rose Book, and who had himself been awakened to the joys of rose growing by it, sent us a bundle of cuttings. Sunny South, Marion Manifold, Red Letter Day, Madame Chatenay — the beautiful names painted pictures for us of roses hitherto unseen. They were by then familiar through word and picture, but what are these to living roses.

The cuttings were already made. Pieces of firm, not old, wood had been cut at the point of junction with the older wood, so that the slight broadening and hardening of the junction still showed at the base. They had been shortened to eight or ten inches long, and cut at a point just above a bud as the Rose Book directed. Father made a nursery bed for them, planted them firmly so that only about a third of their length was above the ground, and impressed on us that not one of them must be disturbed: if any weeding had to be done he would do it. He had often grown cuttings before, and we expected a reasonable number of successes. We were not disappointed. Many of them grew, and still add to the joy of the garden.

A whole year had to pass before they would be rooted and ready to transplant. How we read and reread the Rose Book during that time! How humbly we promised ourselves that we would do just as the writer advised! And what roses we dreamed of! The ground was well trenched on either side of the path, so that the roots would not be confined, as the roots of those first roses had been, in circular wells of

mud during the winter. Many barrows full of leafmould and some of ill savoured manure went into the holes, that were opened long before planting time to sweeten by exposure. A month or more later there was a generous addition of lime. "It's easy to put in first, but once the rose is planted you can only put it on top," someone said. We agreed, though by no means despising top-dressing. Besides, though roses are often described as liking a "stiff clayey loam," it is doubtful whether they would have approved of, or even lived in, the gluey stiffness of our clay, without the rich addition of food and lime.

Long before the end of the year we could see which roses were growing, and they were all too few for our soaring plans. We wanted roses, with arches at intervals, the whole length of each side of the central path, and though we couldn't get them all at once we decided that we would give ourselves the luxury of twelve new roses that year, in addition to our rooted cuttings. We did not wait for Christmas or birthdays as an excuse as we usually had to do. We simply bought them "in cold blood" as Mother put it unpoetically. We talked over the list for days, gradually cutting it down from the large number that at first seemed indispensable, to the permissible twelve, and we savoured fully each happy moment of the planning, like some special treat.

Fortunately we ordered that first lot of new roses (it was in 1922) from a rose specialist, and all were true to name. I do not think that this had ever happened when we have ordered roses from a general nursery. We do not blame the nurserymen. Roses are a sideline to them, and in other respects they rarely disappoint us, but we blame ourselves for ordering from

The "Via Rosarius", April 1929

them, and long ago gave up running risks in such an important matter.

When the roses came they were already pruned, and there was little root pruning to do as they were well balanced plants, with no broken or straggling roots. We had only to sort them out according to the color arrangement already planned and plant them in the prepared holes, spreading the roots over the freshly loosened and carefully convex surfaces, before watering, filling in and firming the soil. We all helped to pump and carry the water, though Father did the actual planting. The soil was damp, but nothing but water brings it into that intimate contact with new roots which is necessary to nourish the plant, so we water plants when we set them, however damp the soil.

We have all of those roses still. Madame Chatenay bears perfect blooms on her gawky half bare arms (she has never taken kindly to us), and Sunny South's crown of blossom is ten feet above the path, Climbing Ophelia must belong to that year, and exquisite Daydream, who shares an arch with her, was planted then. Ophelia got out of hand for a year or two, and then began to look rather woody and drab, but stern measures with saw and secateurs at pruning time seem to have renewed her youth.

Every branch was cut back to a strong young shoot, the shoots themselves were shortened a little, and every dry or feeble twig was cut out. It was hard work. Even from the top of the ladder it was difficult to reach some of the boughs, and high pruning is precarious work when the ladder stands on a sloping path. Thorns check the impulse to grasp the rose for support, and in any case one needs both one's hands for the work. But the next spring and summer's blossoming, the daily unfolding of rosy amber buds, was worth working for, and in any case, though one may be uncomfortable at times, pruning is enjoyable for its own sake. I am inclined to be too soft-hearted, perhaps it would be truer to say too weak, with plants, to shirk cutting beautiful growth even when it would be better removed, yet there is a magic in rose pruning, and fruit tree pruning too, which makes the cutting, the thinning and shortening back a keen and satisfying pleasure. And when it is done, when the secateurs have

been dipped in lysol for the last time and the plants sprayed with kerosene emulsion, the prunings gathered up and burned, the ground rough dug and limed, one views the garden with a satisfaction hardly surpassed when leaf and blossom clothe it with rainbows.

Our plan of a Via Rosarius up the long garden slope was not an ideal one, either for the roses or for the other plants in the garden, and I realise more fully each year why rosarians say that roses should be in a garden by themselves. For many reasons it is best. One may have roses without a rose garden. Bush and standard, pillar and arch are beautiful among other flowers, but if one has a number of bush roses they are happier apart from other growth, and they are also much easier to care for. At the same time our method has advantages and the long path, walled and arched with roses, is very beautiful. The chief disadvantage is that everything else becomes simply a background for the roses when they are in bloom, and when they are bare they make an awkward barrier between the path and other flowers. Still one cannot have everything perfect in a garden as unplanned as ours, and the rose path is a treasure we could hardly part with now.

American Pillar rose, 1936

We have not many rose pests to contend with. There are so many little birds in the garden that aphides are rarely numerous enough to do much harm, and a thorough spraying with kerosene emulsion immediately after the winter pruning (it is too strong to be used on the foliage) and a certain amount of watchfulness during the year, keep them in check. Nothing clears aphides from a soft shoot so effectively as a finger and thumb used with discrimination.

We have only twice had thrips among the roses, but there can be few places where mildew is so at home. There is usually moisture in the air, and during at least half of the year there is warmth as well. It is no wonder that mildew spreads like a blighting shadow on the leaves. We do not wait for its appearance now, but during the winter we put the ashes from our wood fires around the bushes, since the potash in ashes checks mildew to some extent. Then, on a warm day in early spring we sprinkle sulphur under them so that the fumes rising in the noon heat surround the unfolding leaves like a protecting army. This has to be done several times during the growing season, but a hundred bushes can be attended to in a few minutes, and the treatment keeps the mildew from becoming serious, and sometimes keeps it away altogether.

I do not think there is anything else, except black spot, which preys on our roses. Black spot is firmly established on Madame Edouard Herriot. Winter sprayings with Bordeaux mixture keep it from spreading, though they never destroy it. The chief enemy of all our roses is the eager surrounding growth which, if not checked, would overwhelm some of them altogether.

After our first rose purchase we bought a few new roses every June. We ordered the plants and prepared the ground in April, so we had nearly two months of pleasant anticipation. The choosing of them was a kind of annual festival, but we do it no longer. There is not room in the garden for another rose.

Sometime during those early years we first saw Messrs. Hazlewood Bros. catalogue. Thenceforward it came every year, and was read and reread as no novel in the house had ever been, and from it we learned much for which our roses have cause to be grateful, and so have we, who enjoy their glowing response to fuller understanding.

Sliprails   John Rowell

Here ended the first era of the valley roses, for, with that catalogue the second era began. Next year the *Rose Annual* came.

We who had lived almost alone in our valley with the roses, saw the gardens of other rose lovers, hitherto unknown, blossoming in the sunny vistas of our dreams. But they were not dream gardens, they were very real. We pictured the nurseries whence our roses came, and the garden at Glenara, no longer legendary for the *Rose Annual* brought us pictures of it, and amid the overwhelming beauty of a rose show, Father talked with Mr. Clark himself, hitherto more magician than real human being to us, for we knew him only as the raiser of lovely roses with lovely names, Scorcher, Daydream, Sunny South, all treasured among our garden blooms.

We learned of other growers like ourselves, country folk, who grew the roses that we grew and talked of them in the same friendly way as we did, seeing them as beloved guests, whose pleasure of soil and aspect and climate must be learned by slow experience and passed on from grower to grower in the rose talks which the *Rose Annual* made free to all. Unseen rose lovers became our friends. They did not know it, but we revelled in their gardens as in our own. We fell in love with Kitty Kinninmonth, rosy-faced in a suburb; we walked in an artist's mountain garden in the flush of morning; we revelled in blossom among the rainbowed terraces framing a West Australian home. And from every one we learned something that has made our own garden dearer or fairer. Especially, comparing their experiences with our own, we learned to know better the ways and wants of our roses.

We bought our first (and only) standards from Messrs. Hazlewood Bros. They were strong, well-grown plants, and two of the three are still blossoming. Marion Manifold we planted in front of my window. "The picture your mind sees when you say 'a red rose' is exactly like Marion Manifold," Mother once said, and I think it is true. What a rose she is! We never have enough of her. She climbs outside the diningroom window, tapping the frame with wreaths of crimson blooms; she frames the hydrangea bed as one looks down from the nursery. In three places, grown as a pillar, she

overlooks the garden path, and on my standard with its laden boughs, in late autumn or late spring one may often count 200 blooms. Despite the fact that Marion Manifold is not supposed to "do" unless grafted, all but the standards are on their own roots. Two are not so strong growing as the others, and a little more apt to bear pink flowers in hot weather, but I think that is the fault of their position, for the others are not a whit behind the grafted plant in strength or beauty.

The other two standards were Caroline Testout and Madame Edouard Herriot. Caroline's serenely radiant, though unromantic, beauty, gladdened us for years. This year, instead of shooting at once after pruning, the twigs began to dry, and a briar sprang up from the root. Now the plant is dead and uprooted, and we do not know why, unless our old

Anemones, March 1928

enemy, Wind, is responsible for its death. One day the leather which bound the stem to its stake broke off, and the wind treated the over-heavy bush shamefully till we repaired the damage. Madame Herriot, though somewhat twiggy and tormented with black spot, which fastens on the pernetianas at any, or no, provocation, is still a wonder and delight to us.

The garden roses crowd about me as I write, every one for some reason asking to be spoken of. The very fragrant roses have a special place in our love. Pink Pearl and Walter Clark and Daily Mail Scented are chief of these. Most of the roses in the garden are sweetly scented, but these are outstanding. One velvety dark red bud of Walter Clark will scent a whole room, and as for Pink Pearl —one cannot pass the bush without drawing breaths of its rich sweetness. We wonder why it is not more popular. It was introduced, I think, about 1925, but already it seems forgotten. Yet here, where it is half overwhelmed by Golden Cestrum, it is a sturdy, yet not rampant, six foot bush, almost always flowering, and flowering freely. We have no rose with more exquisite pink buds, no rose more fragrant. I have just gathered one bloom from a cluster of twelve buds and half open flowers, and am trying vainly to remember which scented rose in the garden on the hill its scent recalls. I think it is Marechal Neil, but it is stronger than that of the golden rose of so many loves. It has so far as we know, no faults except a tendency to burn in hot sun, and a slight flatness when the blooms are full blown, which is the result of its short inner petals. In almost all gardens I suppose there is one rose which has found the

conditions which suit it most perfectly, hence every rose grower has some love which he speaks of glowingly, though his friends, in that connection at least less fortunate, have discarded it years ago. Is Pink Pearl one of these? Or has she never been really known?

Climbing Daily Mail Scented does not need to be commended now. Its virtues of scent and form and colour and freedom of bloom are well known. Now, in the lull in blossoming that comes in mid-February, every branch is a wreath set with crimson blooms, and it has flowered continuously since early spring.

But why speak particulary of these? Each rose in our path of the roses has many virtues to commend it. Virtues? That is hardly the word, there is a primness about it, charms rather; graces, loveliness, delights. Here are fine gentlemen like Rev. F. Page Roberts, and E.G. Hill and William Orr, there lovely ladies, Madame Butterfly and Una Wallace, Mrs. W.E. Lenon, her perfect blooms undisturbed by the hottest day, and Mrs. Mackellar with her heart of gold.

There have been many failures or partial failures among our roses too. There is Red Radiance, still suffered in the background, but as dull and dowdy as a rose can be, Chateau de Clos Vougeot, so disheartened and miserable that we have given up trying to grow him; Midnight Sun, which delights us for a year or two then turns yellow and dies. Mrs. Phillip Russel is far too subject to mildew for this mild damp climate, but her buds are so lovely that we overlook her starved and shrinking foliage, and even, remembering them, dare not call her a failure after all.

"Dunedin", c.1918

Winters Morning, 1914   Frederick McCubbin

There are triumphs too. What treasures some roses become, partly because of obstacles surmounted in their growth! Three times we tried to grow Rose Marie, first as a bush, then as a climber. We thought that we gave her all that a rose could desire or enjoy, yet twice she faded steadily to death, and the third time the graft was cracked when she arrived (a miserable plant this one, not from a rose specialist). The fourth plant was a Climbing Rose Marie which simply leaped into growth and blossom. Her blooms hang thick on an archway now, every bud is perfect, every bloom delicate and rosy, and unless she is ready to do so she does not so much as open from bud to full bloom on the hottest day. One would think that heat meant nothing at all to her. She shares an arch with beautiful and fragrant, yet sometimes a thought overcrowded, Dame Edith Helen, finer in the climbing than the normal variety, and her nearest other neighbour is Climbing Caroline Testout, who is so lovely that we will never bother with her as a bush or standard again. We do not care for many standards in any case. The bush roses seem happier, and are less expensive. We might have two bushes for

the price of one standard — and who could resist an extra rose?

Lorraine Lee is one of our triumphs. After sulking in depressing and half-hearted commonness for years, she has suddenly begun to grow and bloom gloriously. We do not know why. Surely it is not because she has become shamefully crowded by a bush of pink summer salvia. Kitty Kinninmonth tantalised us for years. She blossomed radiantly, then shrivelled up with rose wilt as if she had been frost-bitten. It was hard to destroy her, but she menaced her neighbours, for rose wilt is contagious, and though we disinfected the secateurs and burned all prunings we feared that the trouble might spread, so during one of her seasons of wilt we hardened our hearts and dug up and burned the whole plant and disinfected the surrounding soil. We could not be without Kitty Kinninmonth though. Mother bought another without even waiting for a birthday as an excuse, and determined to care for it herself. She gave it just the soil that roses love, on the east side of the house, where she grew her special treasures, and it grew on delightedly from the very first, and soon waved blossomy arms above the highest support we had placed for it. It has

The Pathway   A.M.E. Bale

annoying fits of die-back now and then, but only on unimportant branches whose absence is hardly noticed.

Some of the climbers are too luxuriant for the arches across the path. American Pillar has a big arch over a side path to himself, and always has to be cut back because he overflows it and threatens to spoil the beautiful Cryptomeria who is his neighbour. "You don't deserve to have such a Cryptomeria," said one of our visitors, seeing the great rose choking it, but we have built an arch for the rose since then and diverted its streams of blossom to safer ways. Paul's Scarlet, too, wants to escape all bounds, and as for Silver Moon and Fortune's Yellow (which we call the Sunset Rose) — they have a whole hedge to ramble in, and they would overwhelm it all if they had not such strong rivals as Tecoma and Wistaria and Gelsemium. As it is, the blossoming of Fortune's Yellow is the crowning sweetness of the spring, and Silver Moon in November is like waterlilies, and cool moonbeams and globes of foam thick on the tossing of the stream. Her foliage is beautiful too, and we love her, except when the dead flowers and seedheads have to be cut off after the abandon of her once-a-year blooming.

Yellow Banksia is one of the most satisfying climbers of all. He seems to need no attention. We started him well on his way up the oak tree and now he climbs alone, and waves a canopy of blossom over everyone who leaves the kitchen door, then showers them with petals as he goes on climbing faster than ever.

Dorothy Perkins was long ago banished from the garden. The eldest brother, by this time become the Engineer, attacked it one summer with mattock and axe, dragging away the tentacles that crept under the weatherboards, tearing out long trailers that had lost themselves in the grass. (How lovely they had been! I kept away, while he rejoiced in the devastation that the mattock wrought.) We could not wholly banish the clusters of smiling child faces which welcomed Christmas every year, so the Engineer bore away some of his spoils to plant against the farthest orchard fence, where Dorothy Perkins now spreads as she will, in company with Crimson Rambler and Black Boy and Rosa indica.

We are fond of all the wild species of roses, though beside Rosa indica and the Yellow Banksia we have only Sinica alba, who rambles away happily on a fence by himself, and Austrian Briar. No wonder that Pernet Ducher wove such a vivid strain as Austrian Briar into his roses. The rose is a little gem with single cups no bigger than a sweet briar's and the dazzling orange scarlet of every petal is backed with dull gold.

I do not know whether Maiden's Blush is a natural species or a hybrid. It has all the charm of a wild rose. It is an old love, not a rose for the garden, but an eager grower who will make a tangle beloved of blue wrens wherever you plant her. She never grows up. She is always happy and frankly sixteen. May we never be without her presence.

If one grows many roses there are nearly sure to be some mysteries among them. We have two. One we call the Camellia Rose. It is a descendant of a rose that bloomed in great grandmother's garden nearly a hundred years ago. It is a thorny rose with flat deep pink flowers, each one with a little kink on one side like a baby's dimple. The other mystery is "Query", which was sent to us as E.G. Hill. We have no idea what it is. E.G. Hill is a glowing red. Our Query is pink, with just a hint of salmon in it. It has every rose virtue but one —it mildews badly. But we overlook that for it has long lovely buds and dozens of charming semi-double flowers, each on a separate long stalk. One crop of blossom follows another so quickly that it seems as if the plant has a storehouse of bloom to which it can reach down and lift up handfuls whenever the spent flowers need replacing. No visitor to the garden knows it, and no one who has seen it knows the Camellia Rose.

Sooner or later, I think, every rose lover grows roses from seed. It is the greatest adventure of all.

Our seedlings have always been inferior to their parents, but how difficult it is to throw them away. They are our children. We at least may cherish and be proud of them, though we would expect no one else to give them garden room.

Ten years ago, Father grew two seedlings from a stray seedbox that ripened on Frau Karl Druschki. One has never bloomed but every season we leave it "just one more year". The other lived for a season, bore two or three gigantic single white flowers flushed with lavender pink, then died. We did not know then that it is wise to bud a seedling as soon as possible, as many die after their first flowering.

Mother is our most enthusiastic hybridist (with roses) but Father usually has some seeds planted, and many roses in the side garden mark their experiments. There is Frances, with her single deep red flower and tiny pink Firstfoot that bloomed first on New Year's Day. Higher than all, finest of all, is Aldershot, with his long sprays of pink and apricot flowers, and most vicious thorns. He is lovely in bud but very flimsy afterwards, and his growth is a perpetual marvel to us. His highest sprays are far above the roof of the house.

We must leave the roses now, reluctantly, yet not sadly on my part, for the garden calls, or on yours, for "You don't mean to say," one may be permitted to parody, "that you would rather read about roses than grow them yourself."

From the front fence, December 1931

Still Life

Rupert Bunny

Books and the Garden

But the dreams their children dreamed
Fleeting, unsubstantial, vain,
Shadowy as the shadows seemed,
Airy nothing, as they deemed,
These remained.

Mary Coleridge

"They went about from one hollow among the rocks to another, clearing away the loose leaves that lay on the top, and then filling the basket with black mould. Black and soft and wet. But it was easy to dig: and the little baskets as well as the big ones were soon full ... Then Sam showed them how to sift their leafmould through a great wire sieve, called a riddle; so that no stones or sticks or whole leaves might trouble the little roots of the young plants."

Mother read the story to us on the house on the hill, and the little girl, who would be Correa some day, longed to go out into the woods and gather leafmould and make gardens as Sam and his sisters had done.

"Tisty tosty, tisty tosty, all among the flowers,
  That's the way to while away the pleasant
  Summer hours,"
sang Mother, and laughed as she pushed baby in the swing under the flowering passion vine, and the little girl who would be Correa saw children at play in a cornfield with poppies and cornflowers blooming just like the ones in the picture book that belonged to the song. "And," said Father, to a restless little girl at night, "there were wildflowers all along the path,

violets and daisies and pimpernels ..." the names went on softly, more and more slowly, always monotonous lest interest keep the drowsing eyes open, and soon the child who had waked at midnight had gone to sleep in a dream of flowers.

So was the love of flowers set in our hearts by song and story, as well as by living things. Our scrapbooks were full flowers, moss-roses lovingly wrought, and blackberries with the purple fruit thick upon them. All the poems we loved before we could read were full of flowers. "The Caliph Abdul Ramah, in the sunny south of Spain," trod "gardens, with their broad green walks," Abu Ben Adhem saw the light of the Angel in his room "making it bright and like a lily bloom." "The primrose pale and violet flower" bloomed even round the battle of Fitz James and Roderick Dhu, which the little boy who would one day be the Engineer loved to hear told in singing verse. It was no wonder that our love of books and flowers grew together. We know now that either would be incomplete without the other. Because this is a garden story, I leave out the books that have no direct connection with the garden, but others must have their place in it.

It was on my seventh birthday that I had my first book about flowers. It was called *Natures Little Ways* and it was printed in big black print that made even long words like mistletoe seem easy. It told how to watch buds unfold and see the likenesses and differences between leaves, making them like people that belonged to different families; put the story of plant growth into simple words, illustrated by drawings of happy children among trees and colored pictures where daisies bloomed in fairy rings, or a little girl discovered the first snowdrops of the year or looked for bluebells in a beech tree wood. It told how seeds grow, and why the mushroom has no leaves, and the daisy spreads its rosette on the ground while the dodder climbs.

One of our first books was called *Three Little Spades* and it told the story of three child gardens so that we knew them as well as our own. That was in the days of the Children's Garden Seed Mixtures, very early in the story of the garden. We learned from it to sift and mix our soil, to cover it with glass if we would bring the seeds up quickly, to remember to plant our tall plants at the back and the very smallest in front, and, like all our stories, it showed flowers as the radiant gifts of God, to be treated lovingly, and always shared. It taught us also, by ways that children remember, of that garden of the spirit within ourselves,

where weeds grow and must be pulled up, and flowers need tending and protecting with a hedge of love.

Catalogues were almost as beloved as story books. In them no plant ever failed to grow, and all were covered with flowers. While I had to spend some weeks in bed during my schooldays, the pile of catalogues stood on the table beside me. When we were very small we used to colour the pictures with crayons, or beautiful paintbox colours that thrilled one with delight as the full brush turned the flowers purple and crimson lake and ultramarine. The crimson lake was always used up first; it made such beautiful roses; but I loved the name of purple most; it was like violets and kings' robes, and the ultramarine was like clear blue sea (had not Father said that its name meant "beyond the sea") Later I found another pleasure. With the catalogues and a pencil I planned gardens innumerable.

"What are you doing?" I remember Mother asking me one day, and I answered happily from my bed, "Making a garden." I had read the descriptions of every rose, and finally decided to have them all, then listed the annuals carefully with a price after each, a whole page of threepences, and added up the cost, making it real by being so practical. Afterwards, being weary, I leaned back and

Jean 21 months

46

Jean in 1907

planted them in a garden of dreams, and they had bloomed like long beds of rainbows, for garden design was beyond my thought at twelve years old, and the ideal garden was a long path arched with roses, with all the plants of "Finest Mixed" blooming in beds at either side, tall ones at the back and short ones in front. There were many lilies in my garden, Mary Lilies as many as those pictured in the *Girls Own Paper,* and lilies of the valley that grew in a valley in one of our story books. Some of the flowers in the garden I had never seen, except in the catalogue pictures and descriptions, and over these was the glamour of new beauty. I grouped them happily among the poppies and pansies and portulacas that had been my ideals of beauty before the catalogue days. A flower named love-in-a-mist, I thought, must be fairer even than lilies.

The catalogue days are not over, for the fascination increases with years. Catalogues come to us from all over the world, and Father keeps a special deep shelf for them within reach of his armchair. We do not use them only when ordering new plants; they are an entertainment also, a perennial interest, a source of plant information that rarely fails us. When we hear of a new plant we turn first to the catalogues to find out what its flowers are like, to learn its habits and its habitat, its tastes and peculiar beauties. If we know nothing at all about it we turn to the general catalogues first, then to the specialists for more information. Occasionally they do not help; then we try elsewhere. One of the several indexed gardening books may give the needed clue — Chambers' Encyclopaedia describes plants of all countries, and Oliver's Systematic Botany has only twice failed us. The information that it gives is meagre, but it helps us to look farther. If the plant we seek has any fragrance or distinctive smell we know that we will find it in an old book full of delights, *Sweet Scented Flowers and Fragrant Leaves* by Donald Macdonald, a Scottish gardener. He will picture it for us in the words of a lover, will tell us whence it came, and often discuss its virtues, its history, its place in poetry and prose.

47

Sunflowers

Marian Ellis Rowan

Ten years ago I first met Farrar in *On the Eaves of the World* then in *Rainbow Bridge* and so entered a new world of delights. Thenceforth one book was desired above all others, *My Rock Garden* which, after ten years of desire and happy hope, came one Christmas Day with all the thrill of the long-sought.

Garden textbooks have never been mere textbooks to us. *The Australian Gardener, The Australian Garden Fair, Bulb Growing in Australia,* and its two kindred books by the same writer have been good companions. They are as fruitful of dreams as the catalogues used to be, and so practical that without their guidance many of our flowers might not have grown at all.

Edwards' *Rock Gardening* never palls, and its illustrations must have been consulted a thousand times. They might well fill us with despair when compared with our own achievements, but instead they become an ideal, and an inspiration that quickens us to new effort and new hope.

The "garden shelf" in the bookcase is overflowing. Edwards is there and Farrar, and the slim Australian gardening books. There, too, is a copy of Dean Holes' *Book About Roses,* and *Rose Growing in Australia,* which is so much more than a mere book of directions. Mr. Elliott's rose book is next to it. You know the part it has played in our rose growing, and it is still read lovingly, though it looks trim and new in its dark cloth cover. That cover puzzles those who know the book in its other guise. It is a new dress that was sorely needed, for one day, in the full tide of our rose growing, Father sat reading it in the sunshine with the staghound, Big Barri, for company. Something, it may have been the roses, called Father away, and Barri, the gentlest dog that ever loved a child, played happliy with the new toy left within his reach. He was only a baby, though he could rest his paws on Mother's shoulders, his eyes level with her face, and he knew no more of books than a baby does, so we did not punish him for the havoc wrought on the covers, much as it dismayed us. We had to send him away later, to a home where he would have room to run without being tempted to chase motor cars.

Father and Jean

The *Rose Annuals* almost fill the shelf, crowding *The Singing Garden* and *The Garden of Ignorance*, and that most delightful of English garden magazines, *My Garden* into the shelf below. It is fitting that these should have another shelf, for they are not in any sense text books.

In *The Garden of Ignorance*, flowers and trees, Persian cats and sheep-dogs, doves and a child, all live happily together, and Marian Cran, who looks after them and writes of them, is a wise and friendly companion. I read the book aloud to the Artist in the golden light where the sun shone through spring oak leaves, and the likeness of her garden experiences to ours gave a touch of romance to our own experiments. Also we learned many things from her. She told us, for example, that her montbretias stopped flowering because she did not divide and replant them regularly.

"Well," said the Artist, "now we know why our montbretias do not flower."

So we forked them all up and set them in new soil, and the next year their red and tawny blooms waved in half a dozen parts of the garden. We had not room to replant the great clusters that we dug up, but others welcomed them, and montbretia His Majesty became famous in our valley.

When the Engineer sent Mother *The Singing Garden* as a birthday gift we read it with delight, and my first thought was "Why didn't I think of that name. It cannot describe C.J. Dennis' garden better than it describes ours!" Then we gave ourselves to the music of a garden book by the author of *Jim of the Hills*. It is a book more of birds than of flowers, but birds are as much part of a garden as flowers are.

I said that only garden books should come into the garden story, but who can define garden books! If *The Singing Garden* is admitted, how can one shut out Edward Grey's *Charm of Birds*, and if *The Charm of Birds* is a garden book, what of *Fallodon Papers*, wherein one may read, "You want to be in the same place, seeing the trees and seeing the seasons pass over the same trees, seeing the first tender green of the leaf come out in April or May, and then seeing the beautiful color of it in Autumn, and so you may multiply pleasure indefinitely."

Many who write about outdoor things take the garden as part of their world. Richard Jeffries lived in one; Hudson loved one, Thoreau made one, White of Selborne studied one, so we must admit them all among the garden writers. Many of the stories we love have gardens in them, and nearly every poet sometimes wrote of gardens, so the two little garden shelves hold but a few of the garden books, even in this one place.

Shakespeare is concerned more with people than flowers, but his flowers have the quiet and living beauty, which is known to those whose love of them is life long. Perdita's daffodils, Ophelia's rosemary, the "Daisies pied and violets blue," of Ver, the Spring, are all flowers growing in their native soil; that is why they are remembered and loved.

Though I have said that most poets belong to the garden, when I have glanced up at the shelf where more than thirty poets stand side by side ready to open the gates of a world pulsing with beauty, I see that though nearly every one brings some garden picture to mind, there are five that belong to the garden more than all the others. Robert Bridges, who gave us the "Testament of Beauty," and Tennyson, whose gardens are the very "glowing blossom belts" and "crowded lilac ambush, trimly pruned" that we know and try to create; Matthew Arnold, were it but for Thrysis and The Scholar Gipsy; John Masefield, for all his strenuousness, since his gardens live; and Keats, with his "globes of clover and sweet peas". Shelley's gardens have always something of faerie in them, and Browning's are merely a background for his men and women. There are flowers in all, but all are not garden books.

Next in the shelf after the poets, are the teachers, with Plato first of them all. His dialogues are of the streets; Socrates gave little thought to gardens, yet the Phaedrus almost might be a garden book, for the two, who

Jean and Laurie

51

spoke therein of love and immortality, lay on the Ilissus' grassy bank, sheltered by a plane tree, which, said Socrates, "is thick and spreading as well as tall, and the size and shadiness of the Agnus cactus here is very beautiful, and being at the height of its flower it must render our retreat most fragrant."

Carlyle is too full of the love and anger and scorn that burned in him to belong to the garden, but it is Ruskin's native air, and whether he writes of Turner or political economy, in spirit he is in a garden or a fair countryside. Even in the curves of Venetian stones he found the curves of hills and leaves, feeling the unity in all beauty.

And where among the books are fairy tales? The children who come from the garden on the hill loved Hans Anderson, and his tales were full of gardens. Kay and Gerda sat under the roses that were in full bloom, "grown up, yet children still, for they were children in their hearts, and it was summer, warm, glorious summer." Little Klaus told a tale of soft grass and flowers in the river meadows, while flowers bloomed and were garnered in the heart all through the story of the Elder Tree.

Though these are not garden books in the same way as those that are written specially to tell about gardens, the spirit of the garden is in them.

There are gardens in fiction that take possession of the story and are as important as the human characters, and other gardens that are merely a background for the tale, with no more personality than walls and streets, while yet other books one reads without thinking of gardens at all. Who remembers a garden in Dickens? — unless it was Miss Trotwood's lawn, and I do not remember even a lawn that Thackeray created, but flowers bloomed so deep in the heart of Scott that his stories are full of growing things, and his trees and flowers are no less a garden because many of them grow wild.

There are gardens, and the atmosphere of gardens, in many modern tales. The rock gardens in Constance Holme's *Things Which Belong*, the little garden with the hedge, and the Dawnbell, are as real as gardens and flowers one has seen, and the Balsam Poplar that put forth second leaves in Esther Meynall's *Quintet* has the most inward spirit of the garden in it:

"It really is an enchanted spot, and smells as sweet as Heaven!"

"You do not know what makes that sweetness?"

Ursala, the forest child mocked him gently with her eyes. She pointed to the sapling struggling to the light . . . and shabbily adorned with yellowing spotted leaves . . .

"O!" cried Ursala, smiling, and tears suddenly stood in her blue eyes, "And my bare Balsam twigs put forth leaves — God sent them again, when all the leaves had fallen!"

Above all the book of our childhood, of our growth and maturity, whose words have spoken to us every day of our lives, is full of gardens. Its whole theme is the making of the Garden of God; rising from height to height, from the time when, in the first chapter, "The earth brought forth grass and herb yielding seed after its kind, and the tree yielding fruit whose seed was in itself after this kind; and God saw that it was good," to the last when a tree of life grew by a "river of life, clear as crystal," and "its leaves were for the healing of the nations." In it have gardens their highest honour, for its Prince sought a garden in His anguish, and spent in a garden at dawn His holiest and most wondrous hour.

How the Artist Came

On his bed he may lie, and enjoy the whole world.

Sir Thomas Browne

For years Father and Mother and I lived alone in the garden, contented together, with the three brothers coming and going. Then the Artist came to live with us for three years, to leave his impress on the garden and all our lives. In the story of his coming lies the history of the hospital flowers which has walked for years hand in hand with the garden's blossoming.

When the garden began to rejoice in colour and abundant growth, making a world apart, surrounding us, a little uneasiness awoke in our pleasure. We gave much time to it and received a rich reward. What right had we to spend our time lavishly on an unshared beauty, spending work and enthusiasm on our own happiness when so many needs and uglinesses of the world were unredressed?

Beauty is good, but if it does not bear children of joy ever more numerous, in other lives, it dies like a barren tree, not unlovely or unworthy; that, from its nature, it cannot be, but unsatisfying and short lived. Thus, though perhaps more vaguely, ran our thoughts, and so our joy in the garden became incomplete. It was not enough that it gave us health and interest and needful recreation, or that its flowers pleased our friends as well as ourselves.

It gave little active joy to others, and that uncomfortable word, "selfish", began to whisper in the hesitant recesses of our minds.

"What pleasure it gives our friends!" I told myself, but in those dim recesses came a half-formed thought: "If ye do good to them that do good to you, what thank have ye," and then again, "Kind toward the unthankful and evil." But then I laughed. Of course there are unthankful and evil people in the world; one is grieved often enough by the suffering they cause, but they are like the end of a rainbow, real and visible enough, but always somewhere else. Our valley is full of thankful and kind-hearted people. "And anyway," so ran my half smiling thought, "when it is simply a matter of sending flowers, what good is there in sending them to people who are not thankful for them. How much more pleasure they give to the people who are thankful for them." They are not like sun and rain and air, and all the material comforts which do good even when they are ungraciously received. There is no virtue in flinging our pearls, or our flowers, before those who cannot see their beauty. "Let your flowers give pleasure to someone who will enjoy them, and is not likely to have a chance to thank you," admonished my thoughts.

This seemed more practical, and the Canterbury and District Horticultural Society's Hospital Flower Service provided a convenient way of carrying out the thought.

November's surge of bloom had reached its glowing height, and was sinking into December's multitudinous leaves; the summer flowering shrubs were in bloom, bathing the garden in sweet scents.

"Its time to do something," thought I, and said, casually:

"What about sending for one of the Canterbury Yellow Boxes before Christmas?"

"Do you think we could fill one regularly?" asked Father, and

"How could we get it to the station?" said Mother.

"We could fill one once a fortnight, with help sometimes from other people, and send it in with the cream truck," I answered both at once, knowing that they were as interested as I was. So we wrote asking for a Yellow Box, and it came, with a message from Mr. Howard, the originator of the Flower Service.

"I have been asked for flowers for Christmas decorations on Ward —, Austin Hospital. Can you help?"

We had already thought that we would rather send our flowers to the Austin than anywhere else, so we were glad that our choice was directed to an Austin ward from the first.

The box was a temporary one, a large tea box with a movable platform in the middle to divide the weight of the flowers. Soon afterwards it was replaced by one similar to the one we now use, the size and shape of a petrol case on its side, with a hinged lid fastened by a rod. We filled that first box joyfully, lining it with damp paper and putting the most delicate

Garden and gardener, late 1920s

A family picnic

flowers on top, and sent it as directed. Thenceforth we continued to send to the same ward, dependent on the cheerful driver of the cream truck for the dispatch and return of our Yellow Box. Once or twice in the course of the first year there came a pleasant note from the sister in charge of the ward, thanking us for the flowers, but usually the return of the empty box was sufficient acknowledgment, and we expected no other, knowing that nurses are busy people to whom the arrival of a box of flowers is necessarily a minor incident in the day.

Twice the charge of the ward passed into other hands, and each time there was an appreciative letter from the new Sister, with, in between, silence. Then during the second year, there was another change with the usual letter from the new Sister in charge. But it was not like the other letters. It was happily informal and breathing the love of flowers, and when I answered it, thinking the friendly exchange ended, there came a reply like the hand of a flower lover reaching out of silence. So began

the first friendship of the hospital flowers, itself like a flower in our lives, sending out tentative roots in that early letter, but now deep rooted and blossoming.

Later the writer of the letter was to visit the garden, and "Sister's" brown head was often to be seen among the flowers as she learned to know the places to which letters and the flower box had already introduced her, but in those early days we learned to know each other slowly and happily, with the flower box carrying our letters back and forth. All the questions we had wanted to ask were answered at last. Were the flowers enjoyed? Did some awake loved associations and happy memories, as we hoped they would do? Were there, among those who watched them change with the seasons, some who loved gardens as we loved them? We felt that we could send more discerningly if we knew these things. Besides, it seemed as if flowers sent from one flower lover to another must carry more cheer than those sent from stranger to stranger.

We learned many other things. We heard of, and later knew, the Cambridge graduate, for whom carnations held memories; the blind man who still treasured the thought of the red roses he used to grow when he could see. It was not only Sister who wrote. We met, through their letters, many to whom all flowers were dear; the Gardener who made a barren plot into a mass of bloom, the Artist, the Englishman who was the Artist's friend, flower lover, tree lover, book lover, even as he was.

We sent flowers to the hospital because we were not content to please only our friends, and we found that our friends were there. The garden in the valley rejoices to bloom for them and we are enriched through knowing them. Not only "the unthankful", but even "strangers" are like the rainbow's end. We see them in the distance, but when we draw near they are not there for we find only friends. The Artist was one of these, and the garden took him to itself.

"Perhaps," I wrote to Sister before we knew him, "there are some among your big family who have special favourites among the flowers. If you tell me about them we could try to send the flowers they like best." Quickly came the reply with more news of her patients than we had ever had before. Of the Artist she said: "When I gave him your letter to read I knew what he would say, and, sure enough, snap-dragons it was."

So the Artist came into our lives. I have not named him thus because he painted pictures, though his facility with pencil and pen delighted every child who came to us. His artistry showed itself most in fine needlework, and in such crochet and tatting as we had never seen before; showed itself too, in his love of trees and flowers and the growing of them, on which he spent his slowly gathered strength in happy largesse

"Perhaps you will come some day and see the garden and your own snapdragon bed," I wrote while he was in the hospital, hardly thinking the invitation could be accepted, but even those who have been considered hopelessly ill can be cured in these days of wonders, and the Englishman had already been able to return home. One spring the Artist gave up the care of the flower box which he had unpacked for years, left the flowers to be arranged by other hands, the pot plants, long his care, to other tending, and came to our home in the valley.

He came to stay for a month; and the garden welcomed him; the shade under the wide boughs of the oak became his livingroom and the centre of our leisure. During our years in the valley the oak had grown from childhood toward maturity, and when the Artist came it had become an almost perfectly balanced tree with a span of fifty feet north and south and the same east and west. Its lowest boughs were horizontal and just out of my reach, though the tall brothers could catch and swing on them. The Artist's bright cushioned lounge stood under them and there Mother and I took our needlework, there we made glowing plans for the garden, planted seeds and potted plants and found more laughter than our quiet garden had known for years. There Father came to rest on hot afternoons to talk over farm problems and to discuss books and flowers and the puzzles and unrest of the world beyond the garden. The Teacher stopped there, coming home from school, chatting over his day's work and play, and he and the Artist, talking together, built golden hours into the temple of their friendship, outdoing each other in bursts of joyous nonsense, or exploring the deep places of life, all so apt to become simple after a word or two from the Artist, whose outlook was broad and clear, widened by life and travel and the good gift of humour.

When the month ended and the Artist left us, the oak shade seemed empty, but that was only for another month. He had found the place where he belonged, and the oak gatherings missed him as he missed them. So he came to live with us, and now all the garden speaks of him.

The hop vines, arching the narrow path where the dahlias grow, were seeds of his planting, sent from the Kentish hop field he had known as a child. He planned the rock garden pond and designed the sundial. The wooden birds that protected the buds on our bluebell tree were his carving; so were the polished wooden windmills whose spinning delighted the children. Every rose knew his touch freeing it from dead flowers, and many a dahlia and sweet-pea he cross-pollinated and watched and grew from seed.

The trees were his greatest pleasure. He had loved the great elms behind his English home, and the oft traversed mile-long avenue at Aldershot. When illness drove him thence to the milder climate of South Africa he grew trees there. In the Transvaal, ten thousand Australian trees of his planting make a grove where no trees grew before. When they were just tall enough to nod over his head and make a whispering he had to leave them, and the farm he had tended, with its orchard hardly bearing fruit. But even in hospital he grew tree seeds, and it was no wonder that when he came to live in our valley the trees were his delight.

"Some day," he remarked, "I want an avenue of oaks. I think I'll plant the first one today," and he picked up an acorn, newly fallen from the tree that sheltered us. The Artist's plantings were never careless. Each one was almost ceremonious. The acorn grew, and because he had planted it on the King's birthday he named it King George's Oak. He used to sit on his camp stool, characteristically still beneath his broad-brimmed South African hat.

"I'm just watching my oak grow," he would say with a smile. "It will be at the head of my oak avenue," he added once. I laughed "How many avenues have you now?" I questioned and he counted them gravely before he replied. "Poplar, sequoia, atlantic cedar, scarlet gum, oak, cedar of Lebanon, red ironbark: Seven. I think I'll have a house in the middle of them and the avenues leading up to it like a seven pointed star," he said.

Even when illness repressed him again, trees and plans for trees were a constant pleasure to him

"Perhaps," he would say hopefully, after a weary night, "perhaps the Lord will come tomorrow, and then I'll be made well again. He might let me help to make the desert blossom. I should like to be told to irrigate the Sahara Desert and plant forests there."

His strength was always limited, but his quick interest knew no bounds. All life was his province and he looked out on it with happy eyes. The garden was never so gay as when he was in it, and he inspired many of the plans that we carried out during the years after he came.

The fountain and seat (Photo by Edna Walling)

The Hedge

Sun brought the yellow, the green, and the red to it,
Sweet were the songs of its silvery rain.

Kendall

Among the Artist's dreams was an English hedge in Australian ground. Before ever he came to the garden he wrote of it, elaborating the dream as one does when love creates it.

"Plant hazel for the foundation," he wrote, "with wild roses and hawthorn, and oak, beech and willow all more or less cut back. It must be on a bank where there can be primroses and violets, with thyme in the dry parts and mint where it is damp, and watercress where it touches a stream. I was almost forgetting crab apples and sloes, with bullace and wild damsons (known as 'scads' in Kent). Just think of creeping up to it on tiptoe to peep into a bird's nest!"

It was inevitable that we, gardeners all and lovers of the England we had never seen, should long to plant such a hedge, but it was not then possible to do so, and we described our own hedge, between the garden and the Woodland, to him instead. It is not a hedgerow such as he planned, a "little line of sportive wood run wild," yet it is even more unlike a typical Australian hedge, which is usually a living fence, no more. Such hedges are beautiful, but with a beauty more architectural than natural. When we showed the Artist our hedge it delighted him, though it was not the hedge of his dream.

"I want to plant that myself, someday," he said.

Our hedge is overcrowded and overgrown, ever encroaching on the path, a wall of green dotted with flowers. In spring, laurel lifts up its white candles there and May is in full white blossom with roses and honeysuckle and laburnum in clusters and fragrant pink and golden wreaths. In autumn there are scarlet and golden and copper leaves, shot through the sober foliage and waving over it. There are bird notes in its shadows, as if it drew happy breaths that released an undernote of song, with stirrings that tell of feasting and content.

We call it the Hedge because we can find no better name. Somewhere in its depths is the dividing fence between the garden and the Woodland, but it is long since we have seen it. Before the Woodland was planted the west wind swept under the pines and tormented the garden mercilessly. The wire fence on the west side of the garden was no protection, and it was as trimly unbeautiful as wire fences usually are. Naturally we planted creepers to cover it, gelsemium, buttercup flowered, tecoma with shell pink trumpets; honeysuckle, smilax, jessamine, asparagus, to make a curtain of green; hungry akebia, never staying within

59

bounds, dropping clusters of queer brownish pink flowers, purple hearted, from unexpected heights. These covered the fence, but long before they had done so other plants began to share it. We do not remember how it began, but before long the fence became the Hedge, and the home of every hardy shrub for which we could find no other place.

When a shrub outgrew its pot, when a rooted cutting was ready for transplanting, when someone gave us a new plant, the question was always the same. Our garden was full of growing things; where should we put the new arrivals? By the fence there was still ground to spare. "There's plenty of room in the hedge," we would say, until we began to realise that the children we had set out, giving them such abundant space, had grown to maturity and found the place too strait for them.

Roses were the first arrivals. We planted a Fortunes Yellow on one side of the gate that led to the Woodland, and lovely rampant Silver Moon next to the wistaria on the other. Favourites brought from the garden on the hill, Madame Rivers, Saffrano, Devoniensis, were lifted from the rose path to make room for newer beauties there, but preserved in the Hedge, for we loved them. Dorothy Perkins twined pink wreaths through the honeysuckle. "The Bridal Rose", whose real name we do not know, grew up among the creepers and cascaded down again in showers of flat white blossoms.

Someone gave us wormwood cuttings which grew up into bushes of gleaming silver with the bitter smell of herbs, and French lavender, purple and grey, which, when it was full grown, a pair of blue wrens chose to be the setting for their nest. "On tiptoe to peep into a bird's nest," I remembered the Artist's letter, and as this was in the later days of the Hedge ran up the path gladly, with the news for him. He smiled, yet made no move to come. "We might look," he said, "yet a bird's nest seems such a very private affair," so we were content to watch the birds go in and out, and did not go too near.

In winter, othonna bloomed in the hedge, lighting its dark green with bright golden daisies, while down the whole length, carpeting the ground, were violets, long stalked purple violets, fragrant dog violets, nestling among the leaves, blue violets like smiling eyes, sheets of white violets creeping everywhere. I planted the white violets in mellow soil, still warm from the autumn sun, watered them, treasured them, pleased by their delicate blossoms with the hint of purple scarcely hidden at the base. How they grew! How they are growing still! A few years ago I pulled up a barrowful guiltily and wheeled them away. Now I pull up whole plants, almost in triumph. We love them, but we cannot give them the whole garden to revel in.

When the Hedge was young I used to dig between the shrubs every autumn, burying a rich harvest of leaves, and the weeding of the whole was a formidable work, but now there is no room to dig and little room for weeds. There are clumps of primroses among the violets, and forget-me-nots run wild, filling the gaps with lovely blue. There are foxgloves, lifting their wands among creepers and overhanging shrubs; white and yellow jonquils in July, and snowdrops delicate as frost on winter days. King Alfred daffodils come later, with spring in their dancing flowers, purple flags follow, then belladonna lilies, pink and white, smiling at the summer sun. They are overhung and overcrowded by the shrubs, wreathed with honeysuckle trails, yet they always blossom, lighting the shadows, catching the sun.

There are many fulfilled dreams in the Hedge. The long desired Japanese Maple grows there; the plumbago, summer flowering, tosses azure sprays across spiraea prunifolia, which, while still leafless in August, is set thickly with small white flowers. In summer the spiraea becomes a mere background for the plumbago, but in autumn it turns scarlet so that each small leaf is brighter than a robin's breast.

In a corner by the rose arched path that leads through the Hedge to the Woodland, winter irises are flowering. We grew them in the garden on the hill, and as children we loved them, finding the flowers, springlike in gold and lavender, on winter days. We brought plants with us to the valley, where they rarely bloomed, and died after a year or so, without ever having seemed at home. Had we cut the foliage back to six inches long every April they would have flowered more happily, and had we given them a drier sunnier position I think they would have lived, but we did not know those things.

Years later someone gave us Iris stylosa (now called I. ungucularis) again. We planted it in the sheltered sunny opening by the gate, and waited, half fearfully, for it to flower. Surely the winter irises we remembered belonged to the vision that had made childhood an enchanted world: they must have lost some of the light they used to hold! It was not so. They did not fail us. They bloomed above the frost, aloof and delicate, stirring our hearts like an awakening song, and when we gathered one or two and stood them in the sun in a golden cloud of wattle bloom they lighted a whole room with joy. We learned afterwards that there are many forms of Iris stylosa and that this was one of the finest of them, yet, like all the others, so hardy that once established a clump will bloom year after year with no care at all.

We had had lilac for several years before ever we grew a laburnum tree. Then from a sunlit city garden, full of birds and peace, came a baby laburnum, packed among pink-tipped daisies, originally "frae bonnie Scotland," the giver said. We planted the six inch high laburnum with daisies at its feet, and seven years later it bloomed for the first time. Now it is ten feet high and its golden clusters nod through the Hedge at purple lilac blooms.

Even looking-glass bush, which is often despised, has its home in the Hedge, just below the laburnum. We brought it from the garden on the hill for the sake of a memory, a memory of quiet streets and coprosma hedges where children came to gather the prunings, red and orange berried, cool scented, to feed the tethered cows. Those hedges were in a seaside town we had once visited. Our coprosma has few berries, but it is bright and sturdy, a personage of the upper Hedge, even though we have to saw off great branches to keep it within bounds. A Buddleia veitchiana grows up through it, untroubled by its rivalry. Every winter the buddleia is cut back to a few short stumpy boughs, and every spring it sends up strong new growths, six and ten feet high, bearing in summer such horns of fragrant purple as no unpruned tree could achieve.

It is then that we look for the dance of the butterflies, as they answer the call of its scent that comes and goes in waves through the sweetness of honeysuckle and mock orange, warm where they are cool. Like the buddleia the mock orange is cut sternly every year, and

springs up again with redoubled strength. It came from the garden on the hill, and the Hedge would lose one of its chief lovelinesses if it had not the cupped white blossoms that crown it, then fall like snow on the path and fly like birds in the wind.

Through a foam of white veronica, Sunny South roses press upward with the light of morning in their flowers, and beyond them abutilons hang red and orange lanterns over hedge and path. Here in the undergrowth are wallflowers, old plants that bloom at mid-winter, in a warmth of crimson and yellow and brown, waking the spring with their fragrance, and in autumn rhus leaves catch shafts of light on gold and russet brown.

None of us ever planted an apricot tree in the Hedge, yet one spring we discovered a tall one blossoming there, and in summer it bore luscious fruit, adding much to the charm of the place both for us and the birds.

Birds have loved the Hedge since it was young. The blue wrens that nested in the lavender build in the honeysuckle now. One year striated thornbills wove their domed nest in the Spiraea prunifolia and scolded sharply, yet without much fear, when we passed. Later they chose the buddleia, and again a rose. Silvereyes seek insects among the high boughs, and their questioning high notes drift up and down. White-browed scrub-wrens run about the ground and eastern rosellas swing on the

Picnic on the Tyers River, c.1920

Angus and "Fly"

looking-glass bush. Blackbirds welcome morning and evening from the arch above the gate, or rise suddenly from a brown carpet of laurel leaves, crying "chuck! chuck! chuck!" as they fly. They built one cupped nest this year in a bower of sunset roses, then left it, with its three green eggs and built again where the honeysuckle almost overwhelms the double may, pushing out showers of blossom that encroach upon the path.

There are two trees in the Hedge that are the Honeyeaters' special domain. One is the baby fuchsia, the other an American flowering currant. The currant was beautiful when we moved it from the hill, a shrub six feet high even then, but it grew far lovelier afterwards. Now it has grown hoary with age, and we have a rooted cutting ready against the day when the old tree blooms no longer. It is in the only part of the Hedge that is not overcrowded, and as it blossoms before its crumpled bright leaves uncurl, nothing breaks its curtain of lacy pink flowers through which the sky always looks brighter than elsewhere.

Mother's bird bath, which she can watch from her bedroom window, is beneath it, and attracts thornbills and wrens, but the flowering currant has a bird spirit of its own other than these. It was from one of the windows facing this part of the Hedge that I saw it first, a quick and slender bird, rufous and black and white, with slate grey wings. As I watched there was a song, like sunlit drops of rain, a glimpse of undulating flight, a swift fluttering, and there were two birds among the blossoms, slipping from flower to flower like sunbeams, hovering with their beaks in the pink tassels like humming birds feasting.

The spinebills had come to their kingdom.

I watched, hardly daring to move, then drew back softly and reluctantly, fearing that the birds might go, yet eager to share the new delight. I called Mother and Father, and the birds did not leave. We three stood watching them, and from that day forward we went to the window day after day and saw the same picture, and went back to our work and were drawn to the window again whenever we entered the west rooms. During that blossoming they were hardly ever out of the tree, and though they departed that winter they came back in the spring, and now they are with us the whole year round. We learned that we need not be silent, watching them. They were quite undisturbed by our presence, and often, after those first days, I would stand with my hand on the currant, my face among the

Eastern Spinebill

flowers, while they passed, unheeding me, so close that I felt the movement of their wings.

We spent hours watching them, and no visitor to the garden that September was allowed to miss the picture of blossom and dancing wings.

The baby fuchsia was a later arrival, brought home from a garden in the hills. That was when the Hedge was young, and in those days there was but one motor car in our valley. One golden Sunday afternoon its owner called, full of pleasant neighbourliness. His wife and family were seated in the car, but there was room for one more. "Will your mother come out with us?" he asked.

"She has never been in a car," I said feeling experienced, for I had, once.

"Then tell her we want her," he said, and waited.

So Mother went with them, by a road that winds through one of the valleys that enters ours, following a little stream among ferns and trees. She came home with a violet root in her handkerchief and a fuchsia cutting in her hand.

"We found an old garden beside the road. There was a baby fuchsia twelve feet high, and the violets under it," she said.

"A *baby* fuchsia?" we questioned, thinking of its height, and Mother smiled at another memory.

"It grew in my garden when I was a little girl," she told us. "The honeyeaters loved it. We always called it the baby fuchsia because of its tiny flowers." The red and purple flowers that clustered thickly along the spray were barely half an inch long.

Mother planted that cutting on the east side of the house, where it grew so quickly that soon another cutting was taken off it and planted in the Hedge. Both are now taller than the parent tree in the hills. There are always some flowers on them, and probably there is no hour of daylight when they are unvisited by birds. The tree in the Hedge is but half visible. Honeysuckle and akebia climb over it, laurel and apricot and pavonia repress it, and in autumn the scarlet banner of the red vine is flung over its boughs, yet it surmounts them all. The growth in the Hedge is like the child's game in which piled up hands keep moving as the lowest one is laid on top, only to be covered

by the lowest again.

By pruning and thinning we keep the growth from the path, rescue the rosemary from the may, the may from the rose, the rose from the honeysuckle, but the wounds heal so quickly that they are barely visible, and in the meantime the beautiful growth reaches upward, and westward into the Woodland, unchecked. Occasionally a plant is overwhelmed, but usually we notice the danger in time to free the smaller growths before it is too late to save them. In autumn the banner of red vine flames gloriously, and the high scarlet sprays are clearcut and beautiful, then the leaves fall, the vine is cut down to the root (there are red vines all over the valley from the prunings, which root as easily as grass) and the fuchsia is freed.

The fuchsia leaves fall as the golden buds of the gelsemium are bursting, then the tale returns to the beginning, the gelsemium is restored to sober green, the vine waves higher than ever, the fuchsia is red with bloom, while close to the ground primroses succeed the violets. Then come daffodils, forget-me-nots, foxgloves, lilies, following each other in unplanned succession through the life of the garden and the changing of our lives.

The Hedge like other permanent plantings in our garden, does not need constant care. It can be left to itself for months while one is busy with other work, and many other things have been done while it was growing. The making of the rock garden was one of the happiest of these.

The First Rock Garden

Not where the wheeling systems darken,
And our benumbed conceiving soars! —
The drift of pinions, would we harken,
Beats at our own clay shuttered doors.

Francis Thompson

I do not know why I had wanted it so much, or whence the idea first came, for rock gardens were not then common in Victoria. I had never seen one, or known anyone who had begun the happy adventure of making one, and all the books, from Farrar's to Beverly Nicholls', which have sprung up round the delightful subject, were then unknown to us.

Yet the dream was there, to be planned for during wakeful hours at night; to be worked for as opportunity permitted. We had not much tangible material to build on, but an occasional picture in an English magazine, one or two short articles in *The Garden Lover,* a glimpse of flowers growing in the clefts of the rocks, were enough to quicken the dream into strong desire.

Probably all of us who love gardens are rock gardeners at heart, for rock gardening stirs the joy of creation in us; we are the builders of a mimic world where flowers deem themselves at home. For me crannied rocks with plants growing among them, and running water, hold a secret delight which belongs to the world that never grows old. One is almost afraid to look that joy in the face, lest the charm fail and the world grow old. Yet it is always there and it

may be that, for me at least, the desire for a rock garden was born of it.

Perhaps it would not have been so had we lived among rocks, but, in this pastoral valley, with its fields and groves, its wattle girded streams and smooth shouldered watching hills, there are few rocks, and those few are little in evidence. So every contact with rocks had been counted a special joy, not part of the world of every day, and I keep the memories as one might keep a charm. I remember the Correa of two years old building a garden during a seaside holiday, making the mountain ledges with rocks, planting the sand with sturdy pieces of coastal bush. There is the sparkle of water in the memory, sunshine, infinite leisure, and content.

Years later Correa the schoolgirl listened while older children read of slopes "where bunny orchids grew in clumps, walnut brown and biscuit yellow, and the blue-tongues are sprinkled round with buttercups and stars and spiders." Of course there were rocks there. Instead of the school walls I saw a rock-strewn valley with flowers nodding in crannies and sprinkled on the lawny ground that overlies granite.

The same thoughts gladdened the holidays when a child with a mountain pool at her feet and broken stones to build a weir in the tiny stream, played with bright pebbles under the water, planted ferns on the sandy beach and lovely seaweed-like plants in the pool, until the golden afternoon closed. There were voices and a parting, a longing look at the stream, a sudden wondering, "Shall I ever be so happy again?" On other holidays there were hours spent climbing beside a waterfall, wading in shallow pools, gathering treasure of many colored stones glistening like diamonds, precious surely, yet so sad coloured when one took them home. There were other hours spent among silver lichened granite, where there were tiny daisies and groves of "pine tree moss", where rock fern grew under the ledges smelling of cool black earth and scented fronds, or where the granite outcrops ran out into the sun, on slopes bright with golden everlastings and purple wild lavender, and the smell of lavender was hot in the air. There the pointed Red Cypress-pines spilled pollen if a bird but touched them, heath-myrtle grew in the crannies, Nodding Blue-lily in the hollows, and the sweet indescribable smell of crushed heath-myrtle was under my hands. If one remembers places like those one must love rock gardens.

Then I went to the Grampians, a rock garden full of rocks more wonderful than my dreams, full of flowers rich in every charm of memory and imagining. This is the crowning memory, a memory of orchids in nestling companies, and fragrant sheets of thryptomene brimming over the shattered ridges, the frail purple standards of bladderwort trooping down a wet face of stone with moss for roothold, Brush Heath on the summits dotted with rosy flowers, and waxy boronia in the sandstone clefts.

The child of the seashore was a woman then, but the joy of the Grampians was the joy of the rock garden on the shore — only the content was gone. Two-years-old built rock-gardens and was satisfied, but Twenty-two looked at wild gardens, knowing that the most skilful gardener could not equal them, yet, *because* the dear home in the valley was among rounded slopes and clover dotted fields, *that* untrained unskilled gardener was not content, but carried from the mountains an old dream quickened into life.

If we could make but one square yard of such a garden as this; one little cliff with plants growing in the crevices and a pool with a sandy shore, how rich we would be! ran one line of thought through the memories weaving themselves into the throb of the train that bore us home.

That year I saw a gentian for the first time, *Gentiana acaulis*, among a group of rock pinks set in moss at a city flower show. And we read our first book by Reginald Farrar, not *My Rock Garden,* but *On the Eaves of the World.*

Time passes quickly in the garden. I often spoke of the rock garden, but I do not know how long it was before Father came home one afternoon with a load of chunky grey rocks, weatherstained, and many of them heavier than I could move.

"For that rock garden," he said.

Again I do not know how long they were piled under the oak tree because I thought it useless to begin while we had so few. They were there when the Artist first came; and they were still there when he went away the first time.

There was only one spot in the garden where an outcrop of rocks could look natural. It was the long shallow bank above the house, between oak and elm, where our child gardens had been. As the "big garden" had absorbed more time the little gardens had been neglected, given over to jonquils and a few hardy roses and shrubs in a carpet of rich short grass, with a tent at the elm tree end during summer holidays. But one autumn day during the Artist's absence I thought with sudden determination, "Why wait indefinitely for more stones? Start now, and finish when you can."

After all those years of anticipation I had no settled plan to work on, only there stood out vaguely from the mirage of dreams steps leading up the bank, a path, a rocky slope on either side, with flowers growing in the clefts as I remembered them in the Grampians.

The preliminary work did not take long. The clumps of jonquils were lifted easily, and belladonna lilies and white flags yielded to the undermining of shovel and fork. Boiling water commended itself as the quickest way of dealing with the grass, and proved entirely satisfactory. Mother, understanding the enthusiasm of the builder, filled the copper and lit the fire, while I stopped to read over again the few articles in the *Garden Lover* which had been set aside because they were about rock gardening. Half of the boiling water scalded the grass tops, the other half scalded the roots after the sod had been turned. It was impossible either to root out that matted grass or to turn it under the hard ground. The rock garden would have to be built on the soil, not of it, for it had been starved and trodden down for years. I dug a narrow strip, with the aid of a pick in the hardest parts. It was useless to dig much when there were so few stones; besides, I was eager to begin building.

"Well drained," said the articles, and I saw that it was so. Backward and forward from the rubbish heap I carried the two old buckets which served instead of a wheelbarrow. When the barrow is too heavy to wheel, buckets make an excellent substitute, and in those days, when the heavy farm barrow was the only one we had, Mother and I became experts at bucket carrying. Soil, manure, and stones were all carried thus, if Father were not about to wheel the filled barrow for us.

On that autumn day I carried broken china, broken glass, crushed tins, pieces of brick and iron to make a foundation where water would not lie: Two or three drainpipes were bedded in charcoal where they would lead under the heavy outer rocks into the groves of jonquils where the garden was to be extended when we could get more stones. Then sand and gravel went over the whole, and these too were carried in buckets from the heap Father kept for making concrete.

Then began the hunt for soil. We had several heaps of leafmould. I took every one, despite Father's joking protests, and mixed them with sand and charcoal to make a rich layer under the stones. Then the rocks were brought, one by one, set in place, considered, moved, replaced, supplemented by stepping stones from the garden and every bit of rock scattered about the place, rearranged many times till we were satisfied. The Teacher came home from school and moved the heavy stones and helped to carry soil. Mother brought us tea, with sandwiches of cress and brown bread and scarlet radishes, for we would not stop to go indoors.

From a hollow stump, where leaves had fallen and decayed for years, we filled two

sacks with soil and dragged them home: a good harvest came from under the wattle trees, the site of the rubbish heap, now cleared, yielded several barrows full. All was conscientiously put through a ¼-inch riddle. Hard work I found it, but necessary when one's soil is full of broken glass and undecayed chips.

In the late afternoon the stone skeleton of our first section was in place. With the thoroughness impressed on us by every article we had read we rammed every crevice with stones and soil and broken brick, placed our stones firmly, flattest sides down, built up our terraces, and by twilight the rock garden was begun. In the dusk I planted it, a sedum here, Creeping Jenny there, in one cranny a Primula malacoides in bloom, in another a tuft of primroses, here a wild bluebell, there creeping potentilla with its red fruits hanging down. After tea, in the moonlight I went out and looked at it with a happiness unsurpassed by any happy memory of planting or playing, then, when hot water had soaked away the stiffness of the long day's work, I went to bed and nestled down happily to plan tomorrow's work — and woke to find tomorrow come before the plans were made.

In the pale dawn the grass was white with frost, the morning star was white in a silver sky. In the stillness a thrush began to sing, and as the light warmed and increased I quoted, as often before and since, "The world is very beautiful, O my God I thank Thee that I live," and ran out under a red sunrise to see yesterday's work. There was no disillusionment. It was there just as I had planned it, and here was another golden day when I could work in it.

Of course, it should not have been planted so soon. The soil should have been left for a week or two to settle, and, because it was not left, much that was planted on that first night had to be lifted after a time while new soil was added. Yet that was easily done, and how much poorer we should have been without that first joy of completing the day's work.

The next day, and many following it, were devoted to gathering stones. Every brick on the place (for foundations), every stone in the garden or on the roadside, every fragment of outcropping ironstone I could find in the bush and drag or carry home, or pile up ready for the Teacher to wheel on the barrow after school, was gathered up during the next few weeks.

"I'm afraid," said the Teacher ruefully, as the barrow, which had aged rapidly, lurched from side to side on the rough downhill track, "I'm afraid rock gardening isn't very good for barrows after they get old." It is not. That one had to be almost remade.

Warrandyte, 1908

Charles Wheeler

70

The Artist's Kitchen, c. 1935

A.T. Woodward

Load after load of soil that Father wheeled for me from under the trees, bucketful after bucketful that I carried for myself, was put through the riddle, and though one riddle shaken till it was empty had seemed exhausting at first, I could soon work for half an afternoon without undue tiredness.

The making of the steps took a whole day, a day of hard work and great satisfaction. They were to be concrete steps, but at first I was content with board edgings and a filling of cinders. Father had earlier brought home several bags of cinders from the railway station, and these proved invaluable in my rock gardening. Though not artistic the board steps lasted till the Engineer came home for the spring vacation, and laid strong foundations of rammed gravel then mixed a grey mess of concrete to build according to my plan. I had not then learned the pleasure of making and using concrete for myself, but perhaps that was as well. My lines would not have been as firm and true as those he made.

After the first day we did not work without a plan. I drew many during the long evenings, and finally decided on one which filled all the available space and gave me two mountain ranges, a valley, a little plain, and a pool to make. Restrictions of strength and stones and soil, new ideas, friendly suggestions, all modified even the latest plan, so that the rock garden of today is unlike the plan in many ways, but it served as a guide, and that was all we wanted.

Before the spring the rock garden, still less than half made, had begun to have form and character, and the jonquils in the background had burst into golden flower beneath the tent ridgepole that stood from summer to summer. Some of the first planting had been altered and the first mistakes righted. A box of succulents sent by a friend whose city garden was a place of delight, had rooted and spread, clinging to the stones. How they delighted us with their unfolding charms! There was cobweb house-leek, misted with gossamer, sedums, red yellow, and white, which bloomed that first year more freely than they ever have since, little rosettes and beads and pendants of foliage that nestled in clefts and filled up the crevices, and all came from one little box of twigs and

leaves. "When you have planted the pieces," said the sender, "shake out the fragments in a damp place. Every one will grow," and every one did grow. One of the special charms of rock plants is the cheerful generosity with which they increase.

The path between low rocky banks ran into a wire fence partly covered with creepers, and from the first it was unsatisfactory.

"A path should lead somewhere," I said. That path led nowhere. I forgot who suggested a birdbath, but the Teacher made it, and set it up so that the path leading to it had an object at last. It could not be, as I would have liked, a pool gleaming among stones, for there was Bluecap to consider. Bluecap was the Persian kitten, a little prince in blue-grey fur, lovable and beloved, but able to leap with uncanny speed if a bird were near. We could not tempt the winged folk to danger, so the birdbath had to be on a pedestal at least three feet high.

It was made with foundations of brick set round an iron pipe. Round the pipe the Teacher, ever ingenious when a problem arose, stood a cylinder of linoleum, which he filled with concrete. A wider cylinder at the base gave an appearance of solidity, and after a few days he was able to remove it, revealing a grey column six inches in diameter with a convex top ready to receive the bowl.

The inside of the bowl was moulded of clay and laid like a little mound on the ground. A circle of linoleum, three inches deep, surrounded it, and the concrete was poured between the two.

Two days after the bowl had been lifted and set in a bed of cement on the column a thrush was bathing in it.

So day after day the rock gardening went on, and at night I dreamed of purple cascades of aubrietia, of frail rock columbines, of clefts filled with many-coloured bloom. Sometimes it is only when we look back on happiness that we realise it wholly, but it was given to me to taste this gardening delight to the full.

"Surely," I thought, one evening planning tomorrow's work, "these days are too happy. I have more than my share of joy." Not all at once does one learn to take joy with thankfulness, knowing tomorrow will have its grief, and even more hardly do we learn to accept our pain without despair, for tomorrow will have its joy. Across the joy of that time came dread that swept all the happy work into forgetfulness, dread of death, then awakening hope, patient waiting. Then we came out of the shadow into the light of spring-time, and the Artist, who had almost gone from us, came back with slow steps and undimmed smile. Then was born the decision that he must live with us permanently, and rock gardening was suspended while we planned the sleepout that was to be his home. It was to stand where the tent had stood, a little brown room with a gabled roof nestling against the low boughs of the elm.

It did not take long to build. We had Len to help us in those days, a merry boy from the hills, unskilled in carpentry yet quick to work and ready to learn.

"I don't know much about building," he said doubtfully, "I helped me brother build a barn once, but that's all I've done."

Yet under Father's supervision, and with his help, the work was done well. Bush boys are adaptable, and usually familiar with the use of simple tools. So there was measuring, sawing, hammering, and where one day was bare ground, set with level blocks crisscrossed with sawn timber; and, laid flat on the ground, the skeletons of the four sides, like bits of a wooden cage, next morning the frame of the sleepout stood complete on the grassy bank, and Len, whistling as he worked at precarious heights, mortised the gable timbers and fitted the ridge in place.

He surveyed the achievement with satisfaction.

"Well, I never thought I could 'a done it," he said.

Quickly the overlapping weatherboards grew into walls, while Father made door and windows, and helped with difficult finishings. The three-ply lining transformed it from a wooden shell into a room, and the built-in wardrobe and blue-curtained dressing table never betrayed their origin by a whisper of "packing cases". Blue poplin and brass tacks transformed a worn armchair into one both attractive and restful, and thus the building and furnishing went on as happily as the rock gardening had six months before.

"Women always put tacks in crookedly," said the Artist, taking a hammer from me long afterwards.

"Are the tacks in your armchair crooked?" I asked, and . . .

"Most of them," he said, with a little smile.

Neverthless when the sleepout was finished — the walls stained brown, brown matting on the floor, the few pieces of blue furnishings in place, the white bed made, we were very proud of it.

"Not bad, for £12," said Father.

"A palace, a very palace," exclaimed the Artist two months later, "and I would have been content with a shed."

The sleep-out finished, we returned to rock gardening. Three steps led up the bank to the little brown room. On either side of them was room for a sloping rock bank, and where the path crept round the corner and under the sleep-out window the rocks must stop, overhanging it, we planned, in a ledged cliff three feet high.

Not all at once could the work be done. We had to be content with much lower cliffs at first, and stones became more precious than the plants themselves. We had two loads of beautiful grey ones which lasted a long time, for draining material and good soil were also harder to get after our first enthusiasm had gathered up all readily available. So when the sleep-out was first ocupied, the rock garden then eight months old, looked very flat and young. Yet we delighted in its youth, knowing every separate plant and stone, noting each change, the first glint of every bud.

Between the two flights of steps I had left a recess, paved with the flattest stones I could find.

"For the sundial — someday," we said.

It was hard to leave it all just when the late Spring blossom was jewelling the stones, yet in November I went to the Grampians again, and there, where every hour is treasured, every moment an inspiration, the longing for a pool quickened into hope. Where could it be, I wondered, and there seemed but one place. The sundial site must be sacrificed. We might never have a sundial, anyway.

It was dark when I reached home after a fortnight away. It is wonderful to return to the garden at night. The paths drop fragrance, there are glimpses of newly-opened flowers, and one of the best parts of returning is the early morning greeting of the flowers. The lilies kept me on the morning after that holiday. There were roses one could hardly leave, delphiniums and foxgloves, glowing poppies, and over all, sunshine and dew, and the voices of birds. At last I came to the rock garden, where light-footed blue wrens whispered to each other among the early flowers. There was a small heap of stones there, which I had not left, and on the stile under the elm was an ironstone boulder weighing several hundredweight. Father and the Teacher were admiring it.

"Yes," said Father, "I brought it. I rolled it off a bank on to the cart, but it will take three men to put it in place."

The Artist looked through his window.

"It's for the fish to hide under," he said. Then the Artist and Teacher looked at each other with dancing eyes.

"Shall we tell her?" asked one. Then they began quickly, as if they feared interrruption.

"That isn't a very good place for a sundial."

"The sleepout shades it too much."

"And we want a pool."

"And some goldfish."

"And we thought we could put the sundial in front of the steps, and make the sundial place into a pool."

"So," finished Teacher, seeing no sign of rebellion, "I want to dig the pool on Saturday. We have all the stones."

Then we all laughed as I explained, "That's just what I meant to do, only I hadn't thought of a place for the sundial."

On Saturday the Teacher was at work soon after dawn. When the Artist came home from his morning walk with Lady Jane, the black cocker spaniel, his invariable escort, the excavation was four feet wide and eighteen inches deep, with the bank like a cliff behind it. He sat down on his campstool with Lady Jane at his feet to watch.

Sifted sand and cement had been prepared the day before. I brought the sheet of iron used for concrete mixing, the bricklayer's trowel and a bucket of water, while the Teacher lined the hole with old wire netting which was kept in place by a few staples driven into the clay bank. I watched interestedly, and a little puzzled, for I did not then know how difficult it would have been to make the concrete stick to the sides, or stay in place at all without the netting.

74

Survey on the Moe, Gippsland, 1876   Nicholas Chevalier

The workers discussed the merits of "one in four" and "one in five". "One in five, well worked in, with a stronger surfacing, should do," said the Artist at last. The Teacher mixed four parts of sand with one of cement until the cement had coloured the whole grey-green. Then they heaped it up into a great sand castle and opened a hole in the centre. The Artist poured in water while the Teacher turned the mass over and over, never letting a drop run away.

"Because," he explained in answer to my question, "it would carry some of the cement with it, and weaken the mixture."

He flung it, a trowelful at a time, against the side of the hole, so that the netting caught and held it.

"Two inches thick all over, to be on the safe side," he said, as I left them at their work.

In the afternoon I went out again. They were putting the stones in place, setting them irregularly one above another in the concrete walls, to disguise their smooth artificial line. The position of each one had been settled after discussion and experiment before the concrete was mixed, but when they were actually set in position the plan had to be modified. This one would not stay in place, that one looked unnatural. As I went out the Teacher stepped back to view a stone he had just placed, the Artist moved it just a little, turned it round, finally took it away. They chose another, placed it thoughtfully, were satisfied; then the Artist returned to his seat, and Lady Jane moved her tail contentedly at the absent touch of his hand. The Teacher dipped his stone in a bucket of water and drove his trowel into the mixed concrete.

"That stone," said the Artist, "is the top of the waterfall."

"And where is the water?" I wondered.

"Have we not a tap, and a hose?" said he.

There was a cave under the stone. I could picture it, shadowy, with green fronds in it, behind the curtain of water-drops. Here would be another joy of the rocks, where one could dream on warm days of being no larger than the flowers, able to go in and out. It was very barren then, with the wet new concrete around it, but above the water level there were ledges and crannies where one could plant creeping things, and in the cave itself Fumaria was soon to grow.

The Teacher had split a small flowerpot and bedded half in the concrete, so that it made a semi-circular pocket covered thinly with cement. A small piece of wood pushed through the hole in the bottom kept it open until the concrete set. There is a fern in it now, with fronds overhanging the pool.

One cannot make haste with concrete, be one ever so eager. Toward the end of the afternoon they covered the newly-made pond with wet sacks, lest it dry too quickly, and crack. "Don't touch it for a week," they said.

Next Saturday they smoothed and surfaced their work with "a strong mixture", strengthening weak spots, making changes here and there. With much labour the big overhanging rock was set in its place and cemented there, then the work was left for another week, during which I had permission to arrange and plant the rocky borders, but not to touch the new work. There were homes for many plants on the ledges, convolvulus to hang down, sunroses to spread above the rock, alpine violets wherever there was room. I planted stonecrops in the driest places; bluebells and hairbells were set side by side, so that before long they looked down at their reflections like little torches in the water.

At the end of another week the pool was filled, after the bottom had been covered with an inch or two of white sand. We all gathered to watch as the stream from the hose welled over the brim of the waterfall and fell from point to point on to a stone in the pool. We could not then make a waterfall unless we stretched the hose across the garden like a big black snake, but later I made a little stream bed fed by three-inch drain pipes. We had then only to put the hose into the other end of the pipes and turn on the tap. Father had brought home another boulder, larger than the first. When I had bedded my drain-pipes among the soil and supporting stone, the rock was levered into place above them, and a craggy ledge was built up behind it, so that the source of the stream was hidden. When we turned the tap there was a moment's sound of unseen water, then a glint in a cave under the biggest stone, before a trickle crept through the stony watercourse and tinkled over the fall into the pool. That big stone later made one of the pictures I love best in the rock garden. A cotoneaster with orange-scarlet berries crept over one side of it; Arenaria clings and spreads on the straight southern face, above a ledge where hairbells and wild violets bloom, and under the ledge, where the cave is hidden among growing things, the water runs whenever we let the water fall refill the pool.

All this was done some months after we made the first waterfall with the hose. We hardly dreamed of it as we filled and emptied the newly-made pool several times over during the first week. The water was cloudy at first, but after a night of rain it settled into crystal clearness, which showed every rock and pebble on the sand, and reflected bits of green from the young surrounding growth. We looked at it, vaguely dissatisfied.

"It looks so empty," the Artist said, "yet we must not put any fish in at first because the new concrete will kill them." Then he smiled (and those who knew the Artist's smile remember it as one remembers the sunshine).

"I have an idea," he said.

Next morning he took a tin when he went out for his walk, and later we found him washing a dozen tadpoles of various sizes before putting them in the pool.

"I just saved their lives," he said, "their pool was nearly dry."

During the days that followed no fish could have interested us more than those growing tadpoles, with their diminishing tails and undeveloped legs. The Artist would sit and watch them. Mother and I could hardly pass the pool without lingering.

Summer came, with Christmas Day, and we turned on the waterfall, delighting the children with its tinkle among the leaves. The holidays brought new interests, but daily we realised the charm of the pool was increasing as our plantings established themselves and spread.

One day two visitors came home from the hills with a gift for it.

"We were fishing," they said, "and when we caught these we thought of your pool."

In a biscuit tin half filled with water (it had been full, but they had carried it for miles) were two frightened mountain trout, under six inches long, with brown and steel-blue spots on their grey bodies. We had fish at last!

"Henry and Henrietta," said the Artist, and we released them in the pool.

We had never kept fish in captivity, but a letter of enquiry to an expert brought a full and encouraging reply. We floated duckweed on the water; we planted Ribbongrass (Vallisneria), which swayed with every current, making cool green caves. There was a glamour about the pool, a mystery of shadow, the stir and eagerness of life. The trout were shy, so I built a grotto where they could hide. Mixing cement as I had seen the Teacher do, I made a shelving beach on a flat rock above it, and planted the slope with yellow musk. The fish were vegetarians. We had to renew the duckweed constantly, and they ate every "wild water lily" (Ottelia) I planted. We did not mind. We had our pool, with its swift life and surrounding flowers, and we felt richer than we had ever been before.

To anyone else it may have seemed a small thing to build a rock garden and a pond, but to us it was more than a happy experience We had touched through it that spring of wonder and joy which is a child's glory — we had seen the many splendoured thing.

White-browed Scrubwren

Woman in a Garden   Marchese G.B. Nerli

The Vegetable Garden

Go forth; and if it be o'er stony way
Old joy can lend what newer grief must borrow,
And it was sweet, and that was yesterday,
And sweet is sweet, though purchased with sorrow.

Francis Thompson

Mother grew all the vegetables we needed for years after we came to live in the valley, but as we grew older the work had become too much for her, and flowers had gradually encroached on the vegetable garden which adjoined the house, so when the Artist came, most of our vegetables were bought at the town which nestles in another valley six miles away.

The Artist, who had grown vegetables ever since he was a child, was shocked, and told us so.

"It is a disgrace," he said firmly, "to live on a farm and have to buy vegetables. Give me Len for half an hour a day and I will grow all we need." But Len went to more profitable work before the vegetable garden was made, and Major came in his place.

We needed help, and had been able to get none locally, until someone said: "There's a man out of work down at the trappers' camp." We sent a message, and that afternoon Major arrived. He was a big man with rosy cheeks and twinkling blue eyes, and whiskers, and he said he was glad to have work for the winter. We knew later that he meant that he was glad to have a home for the winter.

"No Missus, I'm not a major, never anything but a private soldier, but everyone calls me

Major. I was in the army for years before the war, and all through the war too, Missus; never got a scratch."

Major had virtues. We reminded each other of that as the winter passed and we could not harden our hearts to send him away. He was clean and neat, his little room always swept and orderly; he was good tempered and kind hearted — and sober, because he was wise enough to keep away from towns and hotels. He made friends with every animal on the place, from the latest kitten to Monte, the old blind horse, and so long as we kept him supplied with books and newspapers, his leisure was happily occupied.

"Got any Dickens, Miss?" he would ask. "A great writer, Dickens, great student of 'uman nature; I can always read his books over again."

Yes, he had his virtues, but the will to work was not one of them. Work that should have occupied an hour would take him half a day. His meals astonished us.

"Soon," said the Artist gravely, as he viewed the narrow door to the room where Major dined, "soon you will have to give Major his meals out of doors." We agreed as Major's face

79

beamed in the doorway, before he came out
—sideways.

Major, then, was to dig the vegetable garden.
It was to be quite a new garden on the south-
eastern slope above the sleepout. It was fenced,
and loads of manure dotted over it, ready to be
trenched in. Major set out with the shovel, and
we felt that the work was really begun.

Then the Artist came indoors, laughing
ruefully. "I've been timing Major," he said.
"Three minutes to one shovelful of soil is his
average; then he admires the view, or goes
over to the fence to talk to Monte before he
starts another."

As weeks passed the green square slowly
became brown, while the Artist used to amuse
himself by guessing whether Major and the
shovel would move more than a yard while
he was away on his morning walk with Lady
Jane. Often we thought of sending him away,
but always Mother said, "Wait till the winter
is over. We couldn't send the poor man to
sleep out of doors this weather; he is so fond
of comfort."

So Major's slow days passed, pleasantly
divided by cups of tea. Usually he had nine
cups of tea during the day (and his cup held a
pint), and each one was welcomed in almost
the same words. "Thanks Miss," he would say,
"The cup that cheers but not inebriates, that's
it, Miss. Thank you — thank you — thanks
—thanks — thanks Miss," the contented murmur
of the words followed as I retreated.

In September we said goodbye to him. The
vegetable garden was not then all dug. We
heard of Major again some months later.

"Yes, he worked for us," chuckled Peter,
who sells vegetables from his father's farm. "I
mean," he corrected, "he *didn't* work for us.
We sent him to pick peas, and two hours later
we found him asleep between the rows. He
didn't stay long."

"Poor Major!" said Mother, "after all he was
at the war for four years; you can't expect too
much of him," but Peter looked unconvinced.

Still, we were glad when we heard that he
had a small pension and a comfortable camp,
where he was expected to do only a little light
work in return for his food. We knew he would
not overwork.

"He does enjoy good meals," said Mother

and the Artist looked at her with laughing eyes.

"I'm afraid I can't feel sorry for Major," he
said.

In September I broke up some of the newly
dug ground with the hoe, and levelled it. The
Artist was ill, but he directed the planting of
peas and beans and carrots, insisting on wide
spaces between the rows. To my inexperienced
eyes three feet seemed far too much to leave
between the rows of peas, but I learned later
how much easier that spacing made their
cultivation. At the same time I planted silver
beet, which came up thickly and supplemented
our supply of other vegetables during almost
the whole of the following year, and parsnips,
which did not come up at all. It was three
months before I worked in the vegetable
garden again.

After Major, Billy came. He was not with us
long, but we smile as we remember him. He
was a merry boy of sixteen, quick and eager at
his work, singing and whistling all day, and
never tired. Moreover (almost incredible good
fortune!) he kept us supplied with chopped,
neatly-stacked wood without ever being reminded to do so.

"My mother says, 'If there's no wood you get
no tea'," said Billy.

"Half an hour everyday in the vegetable
garden, Billy," said the Artist, and Billy set to
with spade and hoe and rake to reduce the rest
of Major's rough digging to order. Vegetable
gardening, we learned, was his hobby. The
Artist outlined work to be done immediately.
Billy nodded. "And couldn't I put some peas in
straight away?" he asked, "I got peas in flower
in my garden at home." That was at the end of
October, and the peas I had planted a month
before were choked with weeds.

We were well supplied with seed. One
evening, weeks before, the Artist had collected
together catalogues and pencil and pad.

"Now," he said with keen enjoyment. "I shall
order my vegetable seeds."

His finished list was a long one. All ordinary
vegetables, and some others were on it.

"Peanuts?" I questioned.

"Yes, why not," said he, "I grew peanuts in
my brother's garden, and very good ones, too,
though the children ate most of the crop
before I could roast them."

"Popcorn?" I questioned again.

"Yes," very firmly, "I grew popcorn in South Africa, and it popped like anything. We will grow all we want and pop it over the fire on cold nights."

When the seeds came he handled them lovingly, and sorted the packets into little heaps, those to be planted at once, next month, or in the summer. Then after my first planting, came a long delay, before Billy brought order to the roughly-dug ground, with its crop of weeds. Then the Artist made a careful plan of where the seeds were to be set, and, seated on his campstool, watched Billy go whistling to his work. ("I do miss Billy," said a neighbour, after he had gone, "I liked to hear his singing in the paddocks, and he whistled so cheerily when it rained.")

Once only the Artist visited his garden after the planting began. He came back triumphantly.

"You needn't buy any more vegetables," he announced, "we have a vegetable garden."

I am glad that he visited it once.

He went away from us, after a weary illness, smiling, into peace, awaiting the morning when his strength will be renewed, but he lives in the garden, and we would not wake him from his rest. Meanwhile, we tend King George's Oak and the Atlantic Cedars he grew from seed, the beginning of one of his avenues. We watch the climbing of the hop vine that he measured as it grew so rapidly, several inches a day even, and grow many kinds of vegetables in his garden. The whole garden is richer for his sojourn in it. Though resurrection fill our hearts with a joy transcending the joy of trees it cannot be that the Artist, being the Artist still, could forget his plantings. "Did my trees grow?" he may ask. So we watch them for him in hope.

Billy still sang about the farm during the hard days after the Artist had left us. I was glad when I heard his young voice, glad for youth, and happiness, and hope. He worked in the vegetable garden whenever he had time. "I like to do it," he said, then more slowly, "I couldn't

The family, January 1929

sleep last night, for thinking of — him," with a glance at the empty sleepout.

We had only one farm boy after Billy left us to work nearer home. We do not like to remember him. Major is a cheerful and wholesome memory, though we do sigh at times when we think of him, but the boy from the city is rarely spoken of. He does not belong to the story of the garden.

The vegetable garden belongs to the Artist. He planned it, supervised its beginning, dreamed of its completion. We could not let his work fall to the ground, so his garden became my care. That summer I began seriously to carry out the Artist's plans. Fortnightly plantings of peas and beans provided us with a continuous supply. Lettuces, tomatoes, cucumbers were Mother's care. She had never given up growing them, and it was necessary to

keep them near the house as the vegetable garden had no water supply. "Use the hoe properly, and you won't need the hose," the Artist had said.

We decided that we must have cabbages and cauliflowers for winter, and the first planting of seedlings was made at the end of February. I had never grown vegetables before, or felt any enthusiasm for vegetable gardening, but it had become a point of honour to attain the Artist's goal of "buy no vegetables," so I set to work to carry out the plans that he had made. It often happens that one does not know what work will become absorbingly interesting until circumstances force a new occupation into one's hands. Thus it was with the vegetable garden. The regular and varied supply of fresh vegetables, and the order of the garden became my pride. No gardening achievement gave me more satisfaction than the knowledge that when Mother asked what vegetables she might use, I could answer, "Peas, beans, carrots, parsnips, red beet, silver beet, white turnips, radish and celery, all ready to use."

I began by using half of the ground that had been enclosed. The other half was to be used for potato growing when I became more experienced. The work was not hard if the ground was kept always loosened with a dutch hoe or "Norcross" cultivator. Only it was important that space be left between the rows so that one could work quickly, for the ground had to be stirred after every shower during summer and autumn, even though sometimes it was hardly damped.

The first summer was very hot, and was followed by a dry autumn, yet nothing but newly-planted seed or seedlings was ever watered, and nothing died. Cabbage and cauliflower seedlings were planted at sunset, in holes that had been filled with water, and they were shaded for the first few days, then the hoe saw to it that the first watering was not wasted. The cabbages did well, and the cauliflowers were tender and delicate, though the heads of many were no larger than teacups, and this in spite of the fact that they were encouraged with dressings of a delectable food described in the *Garden Lover*. I realised later that the ground was not worked deeply enough for cauliflowers. The early crops of peas had been

Harrowing Mt. Hope, c.1925

83

trenched into the bed, but they were not far underground, for I had been afraid to bring up the clay subsoil and the mellowed surface was shallow.

By this time the page on vegetable culture in the *Garden Lover* had become of first importance to me, and it was even looked at before the Children's section, long first favourite. Following directions given there, I trenched the spare ground, using all the garden rubbish I could find in the trenches, and limed it in the autumn, planning the next season's crop, as the Artist would have done, so that root crops followed peas and french beans, and broad beans and early peas succeeded the cabbages and turnips.

The flowers were not less beloved than they had always been, but each month's work among them was so familiar that we needed no magazine columns to remind us of it. The routine of the vegetable garden was strange, and without the advice of "Syringa" and the weekly reminders of "Culturist" in our daily newspaper, I should have been lost.

At first I made the mistake of following them too exactly, not realising that the best writers cannot give advice which is equally applicable in all localities. "Two weeks later than Melbourne" had always been our rule for the flower garden, but I learned that we had to modify this from year to year. We had often to allow another week, or even two weeks, before beginning our spring plantings while sowings of seeds in late autumn had to be even earlier than advised, so that the plants would be established before the winter, when growth almost stopped.

These things each must learn for himself, but once observation has taught what modifications the climate of one's own district require, the reminders in papers and magazines are most helpful. During those early days in the vegetable garden I looked for them eagerly, as one watches for the next chapter of an absorbing tale.

Pumpkins and melons are not allowed in the vegetable garden — they are too sprawly and luxuriant to be allowed among the neat rows of beans and carrots. They have their own place nearer to the house. Salad vegetables too are grown within reach of the house, but all others belong to the garden the Artist planned.

His peanuts did not grow; probably they rotted during the unusually wet weather that followed their planting. The popcorn became a tasseled green wall along the east side of the garden, tempting the cows to such pushing and stretching that we resolved never to grow it again, lest the fence collapse under the strain of strong chests and thrusting horns. The cobs swelled and ripened well, but they tempted bolder thieves than the two Ayrshire cows. Every day parrots stripped off the green sheaths and feasted on the milky corn, returning as often as we chased them away, so, after all, there was no corn to pop over the winter fire.

There were a few other failures, due as much to the wet season as to my inexperience, but at the end of the year we had bought no vegetables but potatoes and one bag of onions. The Artist's goal was in sight.

In August I planted potatoes. The ground reserved for them had been dug long before and lain fallow, while I kept the autumn weeds in check with a hoe. It was not hard to dig; digging is pleasant work on cool, sunny days, but I was less enthusiastic about the planting, and when the crinkled leaves came up through a sea of weeds the hoeing was weary work under a hot November sun. Still that was all forgotten when I dug the crop on a stormy summer afternoon. Every plant was a fresh surprise. Most of the potatoes were big and smooth, and the soil broke away from them readily, leaving big tubers and flocks of little "marbles" exposed. There was no weariness then. Does a miner weary when he finds gold? Or a child making daisy chains, as the distance

reveals ever finer flowers? So I, lost in enthusiasm for the earth's generosity, lifted plant after plant, shook out the soil, and threw the harvest into heaps. The Student, who was working near me, admired every special find, and when we went indoors at sunset we took in with us the finest root, a bucketful in all, with several tubers weighing over two pounds, to be kept for seed.

After tea, because lightning still played on stormclouds rising in the west, I went out in the moonlight and gathered up my amber harvest, more than a sackful of smooth tubers, besides those already used. As the Student carried them into shelter, the storm-clouds blotted out the moon.

The garden is fully established now.

Potatoes and onions grow there, with nearly every vegetable in season — beans and peas, root crops, fallow, cabbages, tomatoes — the careful rotation is kept up as the Artist planned and the gardening books advise.

An asparagus bed is the latest addition; the first sprouts are breaking the cold soil now. Last summer we had home-grown celery, too. It was rather tough celery, and not very white, for it is not easy to grow crisp celery without water, still, the inside stalks were well flavored and not very stringy, and the rest made delectable soups as well as preserving the garden's reputation for "all vegetables in season," all, that is, except those grown in Mother's pumpkin patch, which has a story of its own.

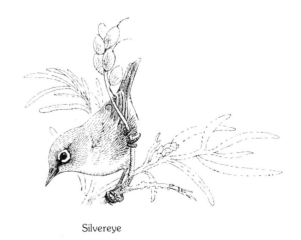

Silvereye

Traralgon Creek, Gippsland

The Daffodils Come

April's in the west wind, and daffodils.

Masefield

"April's in the west wind, and daffodils." It is so the world over. April or September, it doesn't matter which, for spring is in both, and the wind sings of daffodils. "It isn't raining rain to me; it's raining daffodils," is the gardener's thought, and it needs but that warm west wind that often heralds spring to bring him the vision of them. For daffodils come with the wind. Shakespeare put the glad spirit of them into Perdita's song, "Daffodils that come before the swallow dares, and take the winds of March with beauty." Wind ever sets them dancing, for daffodils, the Lent Lilies of England, are not grave like tall lilies. Their smile is the smile of youth and their loveliness is the loveliness of April. "Be glad, be glad, be glad, for winter ends in spring," sang the Angel, "and all the daffodils danced for joy"; that is part of a story I loved as a child, and the Angel was childhood's angel, waking a child at the dawn of the first day of spring.

These daffodils of dreams and stories are always yellow trumpet daffodils. The various forms and colours which hybridists have wrought are very lovely, but our "hosts of golden daffodils" are of one kind only. There are, of course, innumerable yellow trumpets,

and of these the ones we have known longest will be the ones the wind promises us. We may not know their names, yet doubtless they are named; they may be tall King Alfred, or Emperor, with its primrose petals and deeper trumpet, or massive Lord Roberts. Of a certainty they will be some hardy free flowering kind that can be naturalised in grass. The west wind pictures Emperors for me, growing in drifts and clusters here, as they grew in the garden on the hill.

We brought two kinds to the valley with us; Emperor and the double Butter and Eggs, and were delighted to find a big bright yellow double one growing wild here in the grass. We did not know its name, but years later the Artist welcomed it as the "daffodowndilly" of Kentish orchards and village gardens. These three we watched over and loved, dividing them as they increased till we had spare bulbs to plant among the orchard trees and a cluster for the roadside.

One day, driving in the bush, we turned aside to the gleam of a golden wattle tree and found in a little clearing a deserted house ringed round by another daffodil, with graceful flowers and short bright trumpets. The flowers

87

ran wild in the grass, up to the trunk of the golden tree, and round the fuchsias that draped the slab walls. We lifted one clump of half a dozen without disturbing the beauty of the place, and Mother planted them, unflagging, in her garden, against a bush of heliotrope where they blossom still.

Until little more than ten years ago these were all the daffodils we knew, and we were more than content with them. We had other narcissi; half a dozen varieties of "jonquils" (as we called, and still call, the polyanthus narcissus), and fragrant Campanellas, buttercup yellow above their rush leaves, and once we saw a Poet's Narcissus, or, as Mother called it, "Pheasant Eye", but it seemed too much to hope that we should ever grow one of our own.

Then Father and I went to a daffodil show, and thenceforth, though we loved them no less, we could never be content with only Emperor and Butter and Eggs. The show was in our home town, and, though much smaller, it was no unworthy sister of the great shows. There were two there who loved and grew thousands of daffodils; a farmer who grew giant blooms in rich virgin soil, and a girl whom then I scarcely knew, in whose garden on the town's edge grew such a variety of daffodils as we had not till then known existed. Both growers were generous with the flowers they loved and most of the blooms that competed with theirs came from bulbs that had been their gifts.

Wondering and delighted, we studied flower after flower, or feasted on the beauty of dozens together. For the time being the white and pale daffodils seemed even lovelier than the gold. White Beersheba, broad-winged Loch Fyne, Cora and Avolet, with their wide open flowers, exquisite Mary West, were all strange to us. We saw not one poeticus, but dozens; and read the stately poet names on them; we stood silent before Warflame, Bernadino enchanted us; Pink Un was so flawless that we hardly breathed near it. Later the balance swung true; we loved them all, and it was still Emperor that came to us on the wings of the west wind, and Golden City, early and tall, was in the spring angel's arms, but in the first joy of discovery the unfamiliar colours charmed us most. I went from flower to flower with the girl to whom

these were all familiar friends. Once more the garden had claimed a friend.

From that hour I wanted daffodils, hundreds of daffodils, pale leedsii, short-cupped incomparabilis, poeticus, and clustered poetaz, white and yellow bicolour trumpets, exquisite small barris, with their coloured cups. But I could not foresee, or even dream of, the gifts of the next ten years, and a glance at the prices in a daffodil catalogue was not encouraging. What hope could we have of growing these new beauties when single bulbs were priced at from three to thirty pounds each! It was not until later that I learned that, beautiful as the new daffodils were, one could be comforted for their unattainable graces by such beauties as Bernadino and King Alfred at 6d. and 9d. each. Nor were we to be shut out from all daffodils, but these. The gifts that began at the daffodil show with a bunch of flowers and a promise of bulbs have continued ever since, and the friendships of the daffodil garden have increased more richly than the flowers.

I took home that night Warflame and White Lady, Pink Un and Mrs. D.V.West, Mary West and Purity and Bernadino, with great Avolet and noble Cora, and Mother, who had stayed at home, exclaimed over them as I arranged them in a bowl. Gathered in the dining-room we lingered over this bloom and that, revelling in their charm, though it was midnight and the end of a strenuous day. Day after day we gave them fresh water, clipping the ends of the stems every few days, and everyone who came to the house during the next two weeks was taken in to see them. Our neighbour brought her guests to see them, the Student told of them at school; they became famous at every house round about.

On the morning after they came Mother took several blooms into the garden to pollinate the Emperors that were dancing there. Very carefully, while we shielded the flowers, she lifted the pollen with the eye of a darning needle and brushed it on the stigmas of the growing flowers. When most of our Emperors set seed that year (and consequently had few and small flowers the next season, though they recovered by the following spring) we knew that it was from that pollen, for daffodils seldom, if ever, set seed unless artificially pollinated.

Most of the seed was lost because we did not know that while the capsules are still green they burst and scatter their contents. The last one or two were lightly imprisoned in cheese cloth till they were ripe, and the whole harvest, nineteen globular black seeds, was planted in the spring.

"They won't flower for seven years," I said.

"That doesn't matter," said Mother, "we will live the seven years anyway, or, if we don't, we'll have had the pleasant anticipation."

Twelve of the seeds came up, like onion grass in the box, and with succeeding springs the grass green needles flattened out into blue-green daffodil leaves, while the narrow immaturity of the bulbs rounded into promise.

We did not have to wait for seven years, as most of the seedling daffodils bloomed during their fifth spring. They were not outstanding varieties, yet there were several good blooms with the Emperor character very visible in them. One of the best was so like Lord Roberts that we could hardly tell them apart; one was all clear yellow, another seemed to be pure Emperor. With one exception the others seemed to be good yellow trumpets with weak perianths. In some the perianth petals did not even touch. The one exception was a sturdy white and citron bicolour trumpet, on the strongest stem we had ever seen. The flower did not droop or nod, but looked uncompromisingly straight before it. It looked as if a strong wind might break it before it would make it dance.

"Isn't that a beautiful one!" said a little boy two years later, looking at a group of three stiff white and yellow flowers. "I grew that from a seed," Mother answered, "and it has no name yet. I'll name it after you. Its name is John, and I'll send you a bulb when it is time to move it."

A delighted little boy wrote home that afternoon in big, careful handwriting: "Auntie has a John Daffodil in her garden. It is named after me, and she is going to give me one to grow."

When the right time came, John Daffodil, a big round bulb that would be sure to bloom, went to the city and grew and flowered in a pot carefully labelled "John". "That's for me and John Daffodil both," John exclaimed when he showed it to me.

While the first seedlings grew to maturity our friendship with the giver of the flowers grew also. She took me to see her garden, and we stood together looking at thousands of daffodils dancing in the wind. The sweep of their sunny flowers seemed unbroken, though bunches were gathered every day, for hospitals, for children, for friends. I took home a second bunch, and later a third, mostly late flowered fragrant poeticus with broad white petals bent back from their red discs.

"Tell me which ones you would like," said the lady of the daffodils. How could I choose, having such wealth before me! I was silent, leaving the choice to her, marvelling at how little I knew of these flowers whose names were to her the names of friends.

In the autumn we knew each other well, and stooped together over the brown bulbs full of promise.

"Have you this?" she would say, "or this?"

I told her what we had, a few more than in the spring, for daffodil enthusiasm had swept the family, and even the Student, in those days a schoolboy with bare brown knees and mischievous brown eyes, having won a prize for wildflowers at that memorable show, chose to spend the prize money on daffodil bulbs, and at little cost brought us all much delight.

We had then perhaps a dozen varieties, but when I went home that night we had thrice as many, or more. Each kind was labelled carefully in its separate little paper bag, aand we planted them with all care in rows, so that we should not mix the varieties before we were familiar with their names.

We prepared the ground for them as our gardening books directed, digging it deeply, then mixing bonedust in the bottom of trenches four inches deep and covering it with a thin layer of sand before nestling the bulbs into place two inches apart in the rows and covering them with dark loam. "The manure must be placed *below* the bulbs," said the worn copy of *Bulb Growing in Australia* which was always at hand during those busy days. Father spent hours with the catalogues looking up name after name, and describing for us the coming loveliness so that the interval between April planting and September blossoming would have seemed long to wait for them if there had not been so much other garden work to do.

We watched for the first shoot, and joyfully recorded its coming. We saw the blunt points push up and unfold into leaves, and parted the leaves gently to peer between. It was so important to know whether they fitted closely together, or whether there was between them a hole that went far down toward the bulb, with a flower bud dim in its shadow.

When there was a bud we closed the leaves softly, almost as if we had been too curious, and waited the flower's own time.

Then came a busy time when we did not look at the daffodils for a few days.

"Come and see," Father called to us, one morning when an August wind blew the wattle from bud into gold. We followed him into the garden, and there, tall and golden, dancing in the wind, was the first daffodil. "Be glad, be glad, be glad, for winter ends in spring, sang the Angel, and all the daffodils danced for joy."

There were buds to watch every day after that, joys of discovery, tragedies of slug and snail, and at last a host of daffodils in full bloom, with White Ladies like butterflies nodding at the Emperors that had hardly begun to flower. But no day was more joyful than the morning when we saw the first bloom dancing in the wind and rain.

That was years ago, and though we remember it well, all the succeeding daffodil joys cannot now be told or recalled. They run together in the weaving of the years, but among them are highlights — special gifts, whose sequence will never be forgotten.

Front fence, 1940

A year after that memorable first flower show, when the carefully planted rows of new daffodils were in bloom, came another flower show, in which our daffodils were to have part. It was with no enthusiasm that we thought of gathering those dancing children and standing them up stiffly in straight rows in a crowded room, yet there was, despite all that a few enthusiasts could do, so little competition that we felt that, so much having been given us, we must not shirk our part. So we gathered the opening blooms and took them indoors to a shaded room away from danger of hurt from weather or hungry caterpillars. For a week we kept adding to the company that filled the round table with luminous colour and lovely form.

The room became sweet with the daffodil fragrance that is often too tenuous to be noticed out of doors, and the blooms seemed to have a perfection greater than we had realised.

Daffodils are loveliest growing and dancing, but the full beauty of single flowers is visible only at eyelevel, and therefore rarely out of doors.

As we gathered them we referred to the pencilled plan of the rows, and, finding each name, wrote it on a slip of paper and threaded it on the stem. Some were so much alike that without it we could hardly have separated them, others so distinctive that once knowing them we could not forget. As the show day drew near some of its excitement caught us, and we regretted less the imprisonment of our laughing beauties.

They stopped laughing when we took them into that cool dark room, and we knew for the first time the spell of their gravity. We practised wiring them, clumsily at first, but with increasing dexterity, and on the night before the show the children of the spring angel stood in groups like court ladies full of dignity and grace. The thin black wire, twisted first round the seedbox and then round the bent neck of the flower, held each bloom steady, looking straight before it with the three back segments of the perianth making a triangle, its apex in a straight line with the stem, and the three front segments an overlapping triangle, pointing downwards, equally straight. We had learned to twist the wire round the stem until, an inch or more below the flower, it caught and held two leaves in place, one longer than the other, both a little taller than the flower; then, continuing downward, we bound leaves and flower stalk together into a column strong enough to hold the still flowers erect. How we grieved, at first, to so imprison them, yet we could not but realise the dignity it gave them, making each one look like a prize-winning flower in that room where were only its sisters for comparison. The wire was not visible when the flowers stood in water, and we closed the door on them softly, with a last glance of delighted wonder, when all were sorted — here six trumpets, there three incomparibilis (how much we had learned in a year!).

They might have been happier dancing in the wind, but there would have been few to enjoy them. Now they would delight many, and we were sure that, for all their grave dignity, they went with joy, even as we took them with joy.

Next morning we had to carry them six miles, and though we had shallow boxes lined with damp paper prepared for them, we packed them with some anxiety, rows and rows of flowers, not one overlying another.

We had been busy since dawn, and it was still early when Mother waved good-bye to us (she was to come later to see how our children fared) as we drove off with Midge, the little brown pony who had known the town road for twenty years, so that we had no doubt but that she could have taken us there had we left the reins at home. This morning, Father held the reins with a firm hand, and I steadied the daffodils on my knee as we drove through gusty September showers that drenched the wattle bloom by the road. Midge's little brown feet, so swift for all her years, wove a twinkling pattern over the gravelled road, and with every bump I thought fearfully of the daffodils.

They were unharmed when we opened them. Other flowers had lost petals or been crushed on the way, but the daffodils came out unmarked, with only one or two that had to be laid aside because they had been picked too long and the petals had softened in the warmth of the closed box. We were glad then of the spare blooms we had carried with us, though it was with regret that we had to substitute them for the big early blooms that had been our pride. Cora, the largest of all, was too early, we

knew, but we had hoped that the great flower would last for one more day.

The show room was filling as we unpacked the flowers; there were busy hands on every side. Friendly greetings and enquiries passed swiftly, though there was no pause in the work. The lady of the daffodils was there, surrounded by blooms that made ours look small — fair though they were. Her one worthy competitor, come late from his farm, was unpacking baskets of golden bloom. Voices called the secretary here and there, or in several directions at once, and she solved problems and smoothed difficulties with unfailing friendliness. Competition, keen though it is, has never spoiled the comradeliness of our shows, which are the meeting place of all surrounding gardeners: there was goodwill, good wishes, and willing helpfulness in the air. The secretary, called by one, waylaid by another, hastened and unobtrusively directed the work, and still made time to arrange her own entry of daffodils. Those who finished first helped the late comers, and scarcely was the last bloom in place when the judge was at the door. As we left, the room dropped into emptiness, with judges and stewards moving quietly between tiers of primrose and gold, and along the many-coloured banks of shrubs and annuals.

We could not help wondering what would be the fate of our flowers. They were not competing with those of experienced growers, but among the novices, and there seemed little to choose between them and the blooms on either side. We wanted them to win prizes, yet there were others whose flowers we wanted to win too; this one had come a long distance; that one had such high hopes. We pushed the swift thoughts aside, prepared to be glad, whoever should win, satisfied that our flowers were beautiful and that the giver of the bulbs had approved them.

The room was filling when we returned, and each new arrival went first to one remembered spot, seeking his own flowers; seeing the coloured prize tickets but unsure till he approached whether they marked his own or his neighbour's flowers. The daffodil judge, who had known most of us as children, though he lived and won prizes in the city now, was telling how he grew his choicest blooms: the vegetable judge, surrounded by piles of scrubbed carrots and curly lettuces, explained a decision to a puzzled exhibitor — everywhere there were friendly congratulations and disappointment well disguised. The secretary was smiling. "The prizes are so well distributed; nearly everyone has won something; that's how I like it to be," she said.

We had few prizes, but we were well satisfied. We had won enough to encourage us, and though our flowers looked less regal than when they were at home they were good enough to justify the Daffodil Lady's faith. The Student was happy because of his own prize in the section for children's daffodils, where the wise secretary had arranged six prizes of decreasing value so that no one was disappointed.

There were friends to see and flowers to enjoy all through the afternoon; the room became crowded, then emptied again, and I went home with the secretary and the Daffodil Lady to tea, to a room sweet with violets and daffodils, to a quiet voice and welcoming presence, to the garden, warm in the afterglow, which seemed a much fitter place for daffodils than the crowded hall.

We went back after tea, through the dark from the red fire and friendly restfulness to the bright hall, where the flowers too had had an hour of rest in the cool air of the empty room. The people came in the evening again, happy and admiring mothers holding up their babies to see the flowers, fathers comparing the merits of this bloom and that, groups of young girls exclaiming as they passed. Then it was late, and the hall was emptying; here flowers were being sold "for the Society," there they were being given away with ready hands. We brought in the Yellow Box from a room where we had left it, and gathered up our daffodil children, laying them away in the damp paper lining the box. They had done well; some had won prizes, all had been beautiful, but their work was not finished.

The Artist used to unpack the Yellow Box in those days, for it was before he came to the garden. I sat down among all the voices and busy hands and wrote a note to him:

"They may not last as long as usual," I wrote, "but some were gathered only yesterday, and we think you may like to see them all," and the letter that came back told how bravely they had lasted, even after that long day at the show. The secretary came, and brought me her daffodils "for the Hospital Box"; the Daffodil Lady came, with her arms full of beauty for it. A flower-lover from the hills came diffidently: "Would you like to send these," he said, and laid beside the daffodils such violets as we had never seen before, flawless great violets with their own leaves round them.

We talked it over that night as we arranged the golden blooms that the Daffodil Lady gave us after the box was filled:

"It's been a good day," I said, and Father agreed.

"But I'm glad there won't be another for a year," Mother said, and again we agreed, thinking of the laughing daffodils in the garden that would never need to be wired and stay still indoors.

Year after year, thenceforth, brought its adventures. Once we won a prize for the best trumpet daffodil with a seedling of our own. That was a memorable day. The judge smiled as we talked with him . . .

"Yes," he said, "I'm seventy-three, but I'm still planting daffodil seeds."

One Christmas, among our gifts, were two bulbs from the Daffodil Lady. They were wrapped carefully as precious things should be. One was marked, Scarlet Queen, and Scarlet Queen had been the most outstanding daffodil in the city show we had visited together some years before, but the other — "See if you know it when it comes out," said the Daffodil Lady. When it bloomed in the pot where we had planted it with only a question mark for a label, it was pure white. The long fluted trumpet and winged perianth could not be mistaken. It was Beersheba, the marvel of our first daffodil show.

There are few of the daffodils in rows now.

They edge a path in the Woodland, they cluster in the garden and are gold under the trees. The Teacher has been to many schools, and at all he has left daffodils. "He is leaving a path of daffodils all about Victoria," Mother says, but the travelling was stayed last autumn and he sent home "for the rest of my daffodils," to make a garden for his bride. The Daffodil Lady added such a store to those we sent that the garden was gold in September to welcome the flower lovers whose home it is.

The Engineer had left daffodils in the gardens of more than one city boarding house, before he too, planned a garden of his own, while the Student, who was the Schoolboy, takes the descendents of his bulbs when he returns to study, and perhaps some of their gold will survive about his several temporary homes.

The Daffodil Lady still gives her bulbs, and they still increase and threaten to brim over her garden bounds. One year she sent so many that, with the Student at home to help, we began to plan a new loveliness.

West of the house between a narrow grass bank and a bed of violets on the upper hedge, there is a long path, arched with wistaria where it leaves the garden and follows the wall. The wistaria has threaded through the hedge, making a bower of it in September, with clusters hanging censer-like from the arch, fragrant like bean flowers in the sun. Beyond it, hung with its clusters too, a Japanese Maple breaks into young vivid leafage above the violets and joins hands with the Flowering Currant with its pink boughs where the spine-bills feast.

Wistaria, maple, and currant, with the snow of the double may among the plumbago at the entrance to the path, had grown wider and wider, making the path too narrow. We decided to widen the path rather than cut the lower boughs too much. The Student did the work, cutting away the front of the bank and heaping the loose soil on top of it. It was hard work but he finished it in two days, and — "There," he said with satisfaction, "now you can plant your daffodils."

I gathered together all that was needful; a barrow filled with leafmould, superphosphate in a paper bag, a bucket of sand, and the bags of bulbs. The soil in the bank was poor clay, but I made a hole for each one and half filled it with the mould, sprinkled with superphosphate, then set the bulb on top, in a nest of sand.

It did not take very long, and the bulbs will be there for years, so the work was worth while. It reminded me of that first planting, only there the bulbs were in rows, and here they were scattered. The varieties were not placed at random. Under the wistaria arch were golden and bi-colour trumpets, but farther along the bank late poeticus and early White Lady were mixed through the other kinds to make the flowering last as long as possible.

"Just think of them," we said, "when the wistaria blooms!" I pictured the curve of exquisite colour framing the gold, and the maple boughs over it breaking the sunbeams and soft with hanging wistaria flowers.

It was autumn then. In August the tall leaves of the daffodils were full of buds, as the wistaria buds came in their coats of silver scales.

But for two weeks there were no daffodils there. We gathered them and set them in that cool dark room as we did before the show, though these were not for a show. A new joy was coming to the garden, for the Engineer and the Teacher were married in daffodil time in a double wedding. "We want it to be a daffodil wedding," said the latter, "will you bring all you can?" And the Daffodil Lady, knowing this, said: "Call here as you pass, and take all there are."

There were new gardens at the new homes, for they are all gardeners, and, when we who live in the valley garden returned, a new host of daffodils were in bloom, and the wistaria with its bean flower scent arched the path, welcoming us back from the new joy to the old.

Golden Whistler

Pigmy Possum (Photo by Rod Incoll)

The Orchard

Apple orchards blossom there, and the air's like wine.
There's cool green grass there where men may lie at rest
And the thrushes are in song there, fluting from the west.

Masefield

The first tree to blossom in the orchard is always the red cherry plum. When I came home from the daffodil wedding the orchard was white and gold; the gold was of wattle blossom and daffodil — the white was the cherry plum bloom.

The tree was like a cloud, but warm and fragrant and humming with bees. The garden takes to itself new associations every year, and the latest of these came to the cherry plum. I cannot see it again without seeing the Engineer's bride poised in the sunshine on her wedding morn with plum blossom in her arms.

"Is that right?" she asked, and I added a spray here, rearranged one there, then she laid the whole aside, for a little while, not yet the bride, but a girl with her eyes on a sunlit valley where plum trees blossomed like snow and wattle dipped its golden fingers in a stream.

The blossom in the orchard is falling now. The boughs will hang red with fruit in December, and we will welcome the first fruit of the summer and use it to brighten the house at Christmas time, until the Student, plucking the red fruit absently, denudes the boughs.

Before the cherry plum blossom falls the Japanese plums are white, and there is "a mist of blossom on the peach" deepening to a rosy cloud. The later plums follow and the quince tree's silver leaves unfold. Before its pink cups are fully spread it is apple blossom time, and changeful September brings the apple blossom rain to brim the flowers until they droop and spill all their dew, and spring up again.

The Irish Peach is the first apple to show its red buds, following the crab apple in the garden; then the three Northern Spies, and Legal Tender, Delicious and Reinnette and Rhymer, and McMahon's White of the crimson buds and snowy flowers, are all blossoming at once, and the sweetest time of the year is come. Before the latest flowers fall early fruit is swelling: we gather the Irish Peach apples, red cheeked, but half-grown and sour, for cooking at Christmas time.

It is the orchard that more than anything else links the garden to the rest of the valley and before I tell you more of it I want you to picture the valley or you cannot know the garden.

A friend who had come from the heights and deeps and majesty of the mountains round us was telling me of them.

"Is your valley like that?" he asked.

95

"No," I said, "it is lovely, very lovely, but not ..." I hesitated.

"Not heroic," he suggested.

That is so, yet it is beautiful. It is limited by no narrow walls. There are mountains round it, those same mountains which he had seen, but distance softens them with amber and blue, the sunrise changes them to vaporous gold light, sunset pours luminous rose bloom on them, yet when it rains they seem near, like a dark wall, jagged and indigo against a leaden sky, or swept grey with rain. It is thirty miles from mountain range to mountain range, and the country between them is quiet pastoral land. The river that flows through it from west to east, with gum and wattle on its banks, is broad and slow, even the younger streams that come laughing down from the hills run quietly through wattle and willow at the last. There is forest in the land which the rivers divide, with gullies and heathy places where orchids grow, and twilit scrub with moss soft underfoot, but that is chiefly when it nears the hills. In the central lands there are green fields, level near the river, then swelling northward and south, smooth as lawns, with sheep cropping them, or cows in sweet pasture.

There are groves and shelter trees among the fields, with farmhouses and gardens. The roads are tree fringed, the foothills where the green runs up them toward the north, are all tree crowned. "I always think of green hills when I think of this place," some one said the other day, "no other paddocks are so green." And a visitor, looking across the green slopes and the New Forest, which is merely a line of sheltering growth, to the hill of the Sunset Trees, and northward to the bush paddocks over the ridge, exclaimed, "Every paddock here has its trees as well as grass: no other place is just like it."

That may be why this garden is in no way separate from the valley. It is a flower of the same soil as the bush and the grass paddocks are, and seems to recognise its kinship with them. Across the first soft curve of the foothills the New Forest links it to the bush over the hill, holding a hand of each so that the smooth paddocks are as much part of the garden as the garden is part of them, and though the garden has no lawn there is sward round it to rest the eye and give value to the trees.

The orchard that extends the garden eastward seems to spill over the little space of grass that divides it from a blackwood grove, "and scatters on the clover, blossoms and dewdrops." Westward the woodland runs close up to the pines, and the pines hold a green paddock close to them, looking across it to the Wedding Grove and the Sunset Trees. ("Everything has a name here," someone said; but how should we speak of them if they had no names?) Southward the garden reaches out across the fence and scatters primroses and forget-me-nots and jonquils on the roadside, with foxgloves in summer, and hawthorn leaning over the orchard fence. The school children know them, and leave them there, "to make the road pretty," or little Fay from the road's end comes in to ask "if Heather and me can pick the snowdrops?" and even then does not take them all.

By two hands outstretched, the garden seems to link itself especially to the countryside, by the orchard stretching eastward and by the New Forest reaching north. While the inner garden, the garden of daffodils and roses, has been growing, these have grown too, and their growth is part of the garden story.

Australian King Parrot

The tale of the orchard is the first to tell, for the orchard was here when we came. It was a paddock with broken lines of trees running up and down, and the house stood well back on one side of it. There was no garden then, and when ground was enclosed for it four fruit trees were imprisoned with the flowers, and others pressed against the eastern fence. The trees were stunted, and many had died, else there had been little room for a garden at all, but several years of ploughing and pruning, and the influence of deep drains gave new life to those that remained. Crops were grown there for some time. During one summer the trees were almost lost in tasselled maize, once tomatoes lay under them like poppies, and once we grew a crop of beans.

In October, when all the trees were in leaf and the apple blossom turning from rose to snow, the bean stalks grew up like a rising tide, and broke into black and white surges of fragrant bloom. We had not lived near a bean field before, but we tasted its sweets to the full that year. "The bean flower's boon" was no mere name to us. It was a gift flooding all our days. The birds must have known it, tasting the fragrance from far, for we never had so many as there were that spring. I remember counting twenty-three species in the garden and orchard on one sunlit day. That was the only year when we had Trillers living with us. I heard the first ringing trill on a silver morning when dew was heavy on the bean flowers and every separate note in the weaving of familiar

Aunt Kate's, Beechworth

98

Tyers River

songs imaged its bird for me. The strange trill brought no picture to mind, and I followed it softly, watching. It was long since we had heard a strange birdnote in the valley. Mother had heard it too, and was watching and questioning. The notes swept by us as if the air itself were an instrument, and the player unseen. Half consciously as we listened we named the birds that we heard. There were magpies in the distance, and an oboe-voiced thrush, pallid cuckoos that spoke the wistful delight of spring, a butcher-bird lifting the spirit with its crystal purity, wren and thornbill, gay honeyeaters, shrieking rosellas, a spinebill's silver bell, a whistler's gold, the "snip! snip!" of a grey fantail breaking into his soft violin-like song, a Willie Wagtail's "sweet pretty creature," repeated over and over again, with the whistling "sessiewit" of a quail. All these were familiar, and the trill was silent.

"It was black and white," Mother said, "but it just flashed past to apple tree."

From the apple tree came neither movement nor sound, but later in the day I saw the bird and recognised it as a Triller, as I had already guessed it to be.

During that glamorous season of the bean flower's bloom, the singer and his grey-brown mate were daily with us. We knew that they had a nest in one of the apple trees, but we could not walk through the bean field, so did not seek it. Scarcely could a bird have a lovelier home than the orchard was then, with the bean field under and the soft apple leaves and rosy flowers for canopy and walls. During the summer, while the beans were ripening, we saw the fat baby Trillers every day.

"We must grow beans again," I said next year, but the Teacher and the Engineer, who had gathered and threshed the pods one

99

burning December day, cried out against it, not unjustly, I knew, and we have not had a bean field again. It was the last crop in the orchard, and the loveliest. Since then it has not been planted, but has yielded a yearly crop of grass for meadow hay.

In time the bare spaces in the rows of trees were all filled, not all with fruit trees, though they came first. At that time there were more spaces than trees.

"It is such a pity not to plant more," Mother said. "Trees are only 10d. each if you get a dozen, and once they are in they will grow bigger every year, even if we have to neglect them sometimes."

So places were prepared, and the first lot of "Mother's trees" put in. Though they are young they are bearing now, and they fill all the spaces near the top of the orchard. There are apples first, Jonathan, her favourite, and Delicious, which is mine, Granny Smith, bearing hard green apples with none of the delicious flavor for which they are famed in other places, Majetin for the winter, and Statesman and Newman's Seedling because they were commended so highly by those who have grown them. We planted two cherries, Florence, which languished and finally died, and Early Purple Guigne, which gives us snowy flowers and delicious fruit each year; a walnut, a

Interior, the artist's home, c.1930   A.T. Woodward

Our Garden   Ina Gregory

The Artist

Brigg's Red May peach, a Moorpark apricot, which all found the ground too wet for them and died, and have been replaced by other trees. Near the lemon tree of the old orchard we put another lemon, and an orange which is now a round little tree weighed with its several dozen bright fruits, and in other spaces Early Orleans plum, and prune, best flavoured of them all, and two hazel nuts, which refuse to bear fruits, though the tufted flowers are red on one and catkins droop from another. The fruit forms in swelling clusters under the leaves, every cream nut perfect in its green calyx, until we break it and find no kernel within. One tree is tall and strong, the other weak; perhaps it will grow stronger and we may gather hazel nuts, sweet fleshed from our own tree.

There were no pears among Mother's trees, for the orchard was already well supplied with them, but between the little trees we planted a few currant and gooseberry bushes which bear good crops of fruit though long unpruned.

"It's such a good thing," the Student once said reflectively, "that the gooseberries ripen when I'm home: you couldn't very well send them to me."

Even then there were many bare places in the orchard which is big enough to hold seventy well spaced trees. There were perhaps thirty stunted trees there when we arrived, but they are stunted no longer. The fig has put forth long branches that are heavy in autumn with purple fruit. When they begin to colour the red-eyed orioles come, and we hear their liquid cry, "ori-ori-ole," all day long. A flock of currawongs joins them each morning at seven; the birds feast on the fruit for an hour and depart with a chorus of shrill lilting cries. "Coming again tomorrow," they say. Silver-eyes come after them, going from fruit to fruit, leaving only the brown and purple skins hanging, yet the crop is so abundant that we have enough for ourselves and to spare, so long as we pick the unspoiled fruit every morning before the marauders come.

The pear trees give an uncertain crop. Winter Cole and Winter Nelis, two of the most delicious of all, bear bravely, and their fruit keeps until late in the winter, but the Bon Chretiens are denuded by pear slug, with which, in these days when they are so large, we cannot cope, so the fruit is scattered and small. But the tall Keiffer's Hybrid never fails us, though the crop is heaviest on alternate years. It has grown up like a poplar tree, so that we have to use the long ladder, and climb precariously to pluck the fruit, which is large and long-keeping, butter yellow when it is ripe, pineapple scented and pineapple flavoured. It is always the first pear to blossom, a warm white spire in September, and in autumn it is a tapered pillar of fire.

"We want Keiffers all about the place, for autumn leaves," I said last year, and Father and Mother agreed. We haven't them yet, but the gardener's dreams are his delight, and trees long dreamed of give double pleasure.

Years have passed since the bean crop scented the orchard, and now the grass is short and green under blossoming boughs. There are daffodils there, jonquils have been flowering for months, cannas are shooting near the fence, belladonna lilies are in leaf among the trees, for all our spare bulbs are planted there. Then in October the grass begins to grow and another charm comes to the orchard.

White-winged Triller

Birds feeding

The fog grass which no longer makes a fairyland of the Woodland, flowers in the orchard still. In December its bloom is like foam on a misty sea of purple and pink and grey under the full-leafed trees. The tall flatweed flowers, which we call dandelions, though we know that true dandelions never lift their heads far above the ground, come into their kingdom then. Every morning their golden hosts unfold through the misty grass and their golden heads dance gaily to the hum of grasshoppers and the rhythm of flitting grey-blue butterflies. Where the grass is shorter there are white flocks of clover bloom which come with the first dandelions, for there is clover under the fog grass everywhere. We like the clover leaves, each with a brown heart on every leaflet, and scan them half-absently as we pass for the four-leaf clovers that we never find. In the paddocks, where different species of clover grow, we find them occasionally and gather and treasure them for the sake of old tales and happy associations, but the orchard clover has none of them.

Clovers and dandelions have each their own charms. After its gold the dandelion gives us fairy clocks whose frail globes told us the time before we could read figures. They told fairy time, all illusion, but satisfying when time meant little and hours were uncounted in our play. The clovers fold their hands at night and bow their heads on them, so sleeping, leaflet to leaflet, with the third leaflet covering both till the morning, when the tented foliage is spread to catch the dew.

Along the edges too, where the grass is short, red sorrel adds a warm undertone to the shivery grass, and there are red and lavender French catchfly flowers, and scarlet pimpernels, and little yellow trefoil flowers. Cranesbill, with its stork's head fruits is there, and purple Loosestrife and the branched heads of the Mouse-ear Chickweed. We find these, too, at the edges of the narrow paths that Father cuts through the grass so we can reach the early ripening fruits. The grass is tall when the fruit time comes, and its thousands of dandelions laugh with us. One path leads to the raspberries on the garden fence and in the early summer mornings we gather them, heaping red and amber fruit on vine leaves gathered up from the same fence to let sunshine in to the slowly purpling grapes. We lean over the fence and gather bright red currant clusters to wreath the other fruit. We like the delicate yellow raspberries best, but the red ones are larger and give a richer colour to the whole. Sometimes there are strawberries too, white strawberries and red, from the garden, but that is only on the rare mornings when we forestall the blackbirds. Keeping close to the fence where the raspberries grow, we reach the fig tree and gather the day's supply, then stooping under the boughs of peach and pear, come to the early purple plums, and gather up the ripe fruit scattered in the grass. A diverging path leads to the greengage tree, and another, skirting the north fence, where the climbing beans hang, runs to the opposite side and stops at the boundary where pink roses have hidden the netting and flung themselves in bright wreaths on the grass. There is a banana passionfruit on the fence as well, and in summer, when the grass is long, its hanging flowers are like pink water-lilies. Other roses are planted below. They are all strong climbers, but young, so it may be years before they reach the height of the netting and spill on the grass.

The early fruits and pink roses, the dandelions and plumed grass and clovers, come all together; then, after a few bright days, when we hear quail cry "sessie-wit" under the trees, a boy with a scythe comes down from the hills and lays grass and dandelions in level swathes, and the quail fly back to the uncut paddocks across the road.

The boy with the scythe is deeply impressed with the importance of harming no shrubs or trees. He does not understand our love for them, but is far too courteous to say so, and where a pink perennial pea has run wild through the grass he gathers all the flowers before he cuts it down, and carries the little bunch to Mother.

"I thought you wouldn't want me to spoil the flowers," he said last year.

For a day the grass lies there in the sun, and the garden is warm with the scent of meadow hay. Then it is gathered up in heaps and later built into a low stack in a space between the trees. Although its food value is not very great, there is good ryegrass as well as clover under the fog grass, and in winter the boy from the hill will cart it away and spread it night and morning for his cows. Until then the hay stack is a fine place where one may sit on autumn days, tasting the autumn riches perhaps more fully among the warm hay and the fruitful trees than anywhere else in the valley.

The open paddocks are cut with a mower, but the trees in the orchard are so close that a mower could not be driven through, for it is full of trees now, though many of them are still young.

The grass is cut before the apples ripen, and often Father has to put supports under the laden boughs lest they should break. We share the work of gathering them with the birds, and it is good on March days to smell the fragrance of ripe Northern Spies, and gather their big mellow fruits, or pluck the red-cheeked Legal Tenders with the thin bloom over them, basket after basketful to be stored for winter use. We gather them in the cool of morning or late afternoon, and during the rest of the day parrots and lorikeets, redder than red apples, and big currawongs, and slender orioles, take their share. They fly shrieking from tree to tree when we chase them, as we often do, but they know the garden too well to be really afraid. When the young trees grow up there will surely be enough for us all.

Yellow Champagne.

Whitesmith.

Pitmaston Green Gage.

Red Champagne.

Green Gage.

Red Warrington.

Delphiniums, 1928

One of the young trees is a loquat. We are not specially fond of loquats, but bees and little birds come to their velvet flowers and we like the tree's shapeliness and its silver young leaves, its handsome mature foliage, and the soft glow of its yellow fruit. There was a big tree near the garden on the hill, and though this, its descendent, has been once broken and once cut off with the scythe, so that it is not yet as high as the summer grass, we have good hope of it.

Five years ago the first tree not meant for fruit was planted in the orchard.

"Are we going to plant any more fruit trees?" I asked.

No one was sure, but we all agreed that when the young trees should be grown we would have enough fruit for ourselves and the birds, and some to give away.

"Then," I suggested, not sure how the plan would be received, "why shouldn't we plant all our spare trees and shrubs in the orchard?" For by that time the Woodland was full of trees, and the Hedge long planted to over-flowing, and still we had many trees in pots needing to be planted out. There were trees that had been given to us, cuttings that we had struck, gums and wattles grown from seed, and it seemed to me that these evergreens, with the different notes of colour in their

flowers, would make the bright loveliness of the fruit trees lovelier still, and give colour to the grove when their silver-grey branches were bare.

There was some hesitation, yet not much.

"Then let's plant my Little Canada Blue Gum there," Mother suggested, and "It would be a good place to put some of those Western Australian eucalypts," said Father.

So the Little Canada Blue Gum was the first tree of the new planting. It is one of those trees that bring memories with them. Its story is part of the orchard's history, and thus it runs:

To the town in the mountains where Mother was born there came a Canadian, and though his work kept him there, he longed for the forest of his own land, and gathered round him as many Canadian trees as he could grow. Among the mossed rocks of the hillside he planted spruce and maple and birch, and walked there in his Little Canada when work was done. We do not know who gave it the name, it may have been the townspeople of those early days, or the exile may have desired the name as well as the trees of Canada for his grove. It had passed into common use when Mother was a child. The Canadian was not unappreciative of Australian trees, for he planted Blue Gums at the side of his Little Canada. "And," said Mother, telling us the story, "the Blue Gums in Little Canada had larger flowers than any others, and we used to gather up the 'caps' that fell under the trees and make plays with them, because they were so big."

We had two blue gums in the New Forest, but Mother wrote for seed from the trees in Little Canada, which is now hardly a grove, though some trees remain. When the woody cool smelling fruits arrived we realised that the giant flowers were not merely tradition or imagination. Mother set them on the warm hob to open, and shook out the seed carefully, to be planted in her favourite seedling pot. One grew, and was from the very beginning un-usually swift and strong. We planted it, in its young beauty of silver blue leaves, below the Keiffer pear, with a Queen Wattle between the two, and there, despite many vicissitudes, it has grown from a seedling to a tree with its first flowering yet before it.

The Queen Wattle of the same planting flowered for the first time last year, and this year was so lovely in its shining grace that even the big Queen Wattle in the garden did not overshadow it.

In the bottom corner we set a Cape Chestnut. It was one of the trees that Mother had wanted from a child. So was the stone pine, well spaced from it. The town of her childhood was full of trees. All the quiet streets were planted, and its broad parks, with their hills of outcropping rock which sent the streets at queer angles skirting them, were set with Wellingtonia and Sequoia and stone pine, as well as crimson-flowered gums and arbutus that reddened the ground with fruit. Arbutus we had already in the garden, and flowering gums in the New Forest, but the stone pine was reserved for the orchard. It is growing as slowly and surely as the Cape Chestnut, and perhaps in ten years it may bear among its dark needles cones as big as pineapples and seeds as big and sweet as hazel nuts, just as they grew on the stone pines in that mountain town.

Already there was a pointed She-oak near the orchard fence, with several young gums beside it, and to fill a space among them we moved a white hawthorn bush that was growing too big for its place near the door. We moved it doubtfully, knowing it too large, but it throve from the first, reaching out branches on every side. This was all the first planting, to which succeeding years added much.

During the next autumn I gathered up all the young trees in pots and distributed them about the orchard, trying to imagine them when they should be grown. They are yet far from maturity, but four years have changed the two six-inch-high golden wattles below the plum trees into blythe young trees with golden crowns. One, with broad leaves and grey-green stems, came from our own hills; the other, sickle-foliaged, scarlet branched, came from Mildura, yet seems happy in our wetter climate. The Varnish and Long-leaf Acacias that stand together were bowed down with bloom this year; the branches of the gum above the Little Canada tree were soft with pale pink blossom, and now the Wirilda above the Keiffer pear is shining through the rain, a lovely tree with blue-green leaves and primrose

flowers. Others have grown more slowly. The Weeping Pittosporum, which was planted at the same time as the wattles, is still living, and still under a foot high. There are others that have grown little more, though few have died. Twelve wattles bloomed in the orchard this year, and all belong to that planting. There are tall shrubs as well, and one now heavy with orange flowers is like a wide golden bouquet hardly three feet above the grass.

Each year sees more trees planted. This year it was two young Japanese Maples with delicate leaves; last year I set a weeping willow. There are young lilacs and flowering plums, with cypress-pine and wattle and pyracantha, along the fence near the hawthorn tree, and michaelmas daisies grow wild under the apple trees. There is no room for more trees, though we may add bushes from time to time.

There is still some semblence of rows about the planting, for the fruit trees must not be overcrowded, and the grass must be cut, but all along the roadside fence we plant with no regard for space or formality. There is to be a thicket there, which, though it is scattered now, may yet be as close and flowery as the hedge.

Few people visit the orchard, for it is not flowery, except in mid-spring, but to us, the garden makers, it is a place for happy wandering. We go there for a moment, to gather fruit, to plant a shrub, to prune, to set a bulb, and go lovingly from tree to tree in happy forgetfulness of time, counting hours by the dandelion clocks that give fairy measure.

Garden Adventures

Trouble and laughter, death and wedding bell,
Birth, and their worship's glad solemnities,
All through the village life like music well
Graced by its singing birds and blossomed trees.

J.G.

All who come to the garden leave some memory to enrich the pattern that is its life.

"Here I stay," I remember writing to a friend, "like a spider in its web, waiting for adventures to come to me. The garden brings them all." Many had visited the garden that week, and I thought back over them. "Could we have some flowers for baby's grave?" asked a sad young girl. I went out with her in the lightly falling rain, gathering spring flowers, young flowers that belong to children, newly opened ones that have known the joy of life but not its shadows, and she took them with quiet thanks, almost smiling. She came again, weeks later, for more flowers, but her gravity was not wholly sad, and she could smile. "Doctor said that I must adopt a baby if I wanted one," she said, slowly, "so we got a little boy a month ago." The dawn of joy was in her voice. "He's such a bonnie boy," she said, "he's that happy and lively I've little time to think of anything else." The sorrow was not dead, but hope and love and baby laughter had charmed it almost to sleep.

Another girl came, rosy faced, with happy eyes. "Joe's being married today," she told us, with a ripple of excitement in her voice, "and everything's ready, and the bouquets made, but mother hasn't any flowers, and I knew you wouldn't mind ..."

Mother had already brought the scissors, and we went happily into the garden together. We looked at all the bright growing things, lilac for maidenhood, pansies for thoughts, roses — what were roses for but all the fullest hours of life? So we gathered roses, velvet red and dewy pink, and gold like the sunshine of hope that should light a wedding day, and laid them together, with maidenhair, in the soft paper that Mother had put ready. How much richer the garden was for the happy young voice that called goodbye. "Mother will love them," she said, "and we thank you so much." "We like you to have them," we said, waving at the turn of the road, and went back through the garden gate, feeling that she had given us part in the happy wonder of her day.

That week also I wove a funeral wreath, yet not altogether sadly, for death had come softly, to heal and not to wound, closing aged eyes in the sleep that is sweet at a long day's end. "How she would love them," I thought, gathering the flowers, and, "how she will love them when she sees them again and has lost all her weariness."

"Gipsy", "Polly" and the butter wagon, 1919

Soon afterwards there came other news, and we three, standing in the garden rejoiced over it. "One has only to wait for adventures in a garden," I thought, "and everyhing comes: wedding and death and childhood," for I remembered the children who three days before had asked for "just one, where it won't show, to take to school"; who, given their choice of the whole garden, had gone smilingly with wattle blossom and daffodils and a spray of the bluebell tree, and "Irises, because it is my name," said the little girl who chose last. It seemed right that a birthday should come next, and the news that gladdened us told us of the birth of a baby girl. She needed no flowers, but they could carry our love and delight to her mother, so I gathered dewy late violets and packed them in a box with their own leaves.

Our flowers seemed to give us some part in everything. They were always ready to speak for us when we had few other words, and whenever we sent them as our messenger it seemed as if they gave us a share in a new experience.

When, in the level early sunshine which is the joyfullest light of the day, I gathered birthday flowers, my own happy birthdays lived again. I chose the blooms lingeringly, wondering how much of all they said to me, they would tell to the girl who was twenty-one next day; rosebuds (would they last?), pansies, not only for thoughts, but because they always smile, shy violets which never fear the frost, lilac and wistaria for the sweetness in them, apple blossom because under its daintiness is the growing fruit, daffodils, who are the angels of spring and youth. I packed them up and sent them away, having had more than my share of joy in them, and if the birthday gift meant less to the one who received it than to me I did not care, knowing that her day would be gladder for them.

The hospital flower box has its own story in the tale of friends that the garden has made, but these other happy occasions that enrich our lives are innumerable. It is not only for youth that we gather flowers, and one who is not young has a special place in our garden memories. She has never seen it. She lives in the city among drab houses. The children whom she taught at school sometimes gave her flowers, or young fellow teachers thought of her and brought her a bunch of daffodils or a cluster of fragrant stock, for she was always frail, and tired with the care of two brothers and a mother who had been ill for years, so that

when she was not at school she had no strength or leisure for more than pot plant gardening. Though she was weary she hardly spoke of it; even when she was sad she would look up at you with clear eyes like a child's, and tell you, with the keenest enjoyment, a story that ended in a joke, finishing abruptly, so that the silence seemed to laugh with you. At last she found that her strength would bear her no farther, and leave of absence, which carried her to retirement, meant returning to housekeeping and nursing, laughing in darkened rooms, though she loved light, wearing a spray of bright colour on her frock because colour was so dear to her, overflowing with gratitude to the brother who spared from each week two hours to spend with his mother while she went rejoicing to the Sunday afternoon service.

"Everyone's so good to me," she said.

Galbraiths at Bulga Park

111

Prostanthera

Daisy Wood

Because our garden brimmed with flowers and she could not come to it, I sent some to her. Twenty-one may not know the language of flowers, but to sixty it is clear and living. I had gathered them carefully, intending that some should have special meaning for her, yet I had not knowingly put into them all the riches that she found there. Every one spoke to her, and she told their tale over delightedly in her letter, pansies for thoughts, fern for constancy: "and I am sure you put the snowdrop on top because it means hope, and the rose because it means love," and again, "I do not know the meanings of the Australian wildflowers, but they gave me more joy than you could have guessed. They used to grow on the hill below our home ..."

For such seeing eyes the flowers need no written message, yet one does not look for all to know the language of flowers which she knew as a girl, but which is only a shadowy lore to me, so most of the flowers that go out from the garden speak only through their beauty and fragrance, and if there is more to be said than flowers can tell, it must be by written word.

All the joy of the garden is not in giving. Receiving has no mean part in it, and we have all the acquisitiveness of our Scottish ancestors. We prefer to acquire honestly, which perhaps they did not, but if there is some ripe seed bursting through a fence beside the street we might not resist the temptation to gather some, or, if among the weeds flung out on a rubbish heap we found a stray iris root, over-niceness would not force us to leave it there.

When the stolen sweet proves to be something that we already have we say, "Well, anyway, it was too lovely to waste," and when it is new we all gloat over it, and congratulate ourselves as the highlanders used to do over their stolen cattle. Nevertheless, the flowers that are the gifts of friends give us more delight. One may take the seed that falls through a stranger's fence, but it has no personality. One cannot, unless it is offered, take seed from a friend's garden, but the seed that is given thence has the personality of the whole garden in it, linking it to one's own, as a friend's gift of flowers has in it more than the bloom's own loveliness, being warm with friendship. Giving and receiving, offering and exchanging, have so large a part in the friendships of gardeners that no one could, or would balance the friendly indebtedness. Perhaps we have a new rock plant, flourishing gloriously, as rock plants do if they like their home, and someone, seeing it, exclaims over its beauty. With what satisfaction we offer roots or cuttings, glad to think that we can add something to a garden that seems already complete. Or a new home is being made, a new garden planned, and we gather together plants and bulbs for it, feeling in ourselves all the joy of creating it, picturing its drifts of daffodils, its nooks and borders, its springing trees, experiencing all the joy of planning and planting, yet leaving the real gardenmaker no poorer.

Or we come home from another garden with treasured plants in our hands, and there is in them, then and all their lives, not only their beauty, but the friendship that gave them, with all the memories of the day when they came and the garden whence they were taken and the generous hands that pressed them into ours.

More than once we have been given daphne cuttings, always with some fragrant associations. One of these is in bud now, by the kitchen door. It is Mother's triumph. We brought a big one in a tub when we came to live here, and it bloomed freely for years. Then scale insects attacked it, and scale is one of the daphne's two greatest enemies. Before we realised what had happened it was so weak that we could not save it. It had escaped the other danger, imperfect drainage, which is usually the cause when a treasured daphne dies, and had we noticed the scale in time we could have saved it, for we could have picked off the first attackers before the bark was destroyed, or if it was too late for that have painted over all the stalks with thin starch and left it for a few days. The starch treatment is very effective, but one has to wash it off before it has been on for a week, so the plant can breathe. Alas, we noticed nothing until the little creatures under their flat brown covers, so hard to see as they lie close to the brown bark, had sapped the strength of the plant beyond recovery.

We tried drastic pruning as a last resort, but there were no shoots from the ruined boughs.

For years after that we had no daphne, and there is nothing that takes its place. One that was given to us was planted out of doors, and after one winter its leaves turned yellow and it died. We did not then know that no daphne can stand a poorly drained or very wet position in winter. We have since realised that in this Gippsland valley, where everything out of doors is saturated from June to October, it is better to grow daphne in a tub than to risk its life in wet ground.

When the glass was first lifted the cutting had grown so tall that the top leaves were bent against their prison. Carefully it was hardened. First the glass was lifted a little, then wholly on warm days, but replaced at night. After a week or two it was left off altogether, and the shoot soon grew so tall that it was impossible to cover it. It was moved, without breaking the ball of earth, into successively larger pots, and when it was two years old its strong, unbranched stem was eighteen inches high. We began to fear that it would go up like Jack's beanstalk without branching at all.

"Suppose I nip off the top to encourage it to branch," suggested Father, with a teasing glance at Mother.

"No," said Mother, very firmly, "it would die of discouragement if you nipped off that beautiful leafy tip. It's going to flower this winter."

"And exhaust itself?" questioned Father, smiling.

"And shoot out all round the flower, like they always do," said Mother.

Mother never gave up hope of growing a daphne. Several cuttings were planted, but met with various mishaps, or made no growth, until three years ago when a sturdy little cutting began to grow tall. Mother had planted it in sand which filled a hole in the middle of a pot full of sandy loam. She planted it firmly, and pressed a glass tumbler down over it, enclosing it as if in a bell glass. For a year the glass was not moved. It was kept moist either by watering round the edge of the glass, or plunging the whole pot in water nearly to the rim; but it needed little watering as, though it could not be allowed to dry out altogether, it would have died had it been kept wet.

Flowers, 1946

Ludmilla Meilerts

She was right. Toward the end of the winter red buds pressed the leaves apart. At the same time a minute pointed shoot at the base of every leaf indicated that the daphne was going to branch after all.

What a flower-head it was! All the strength of that great erect stem helped to build it, and the cluster of flowers was three inches in diameter. The separate flowers were almost twice as large as normal blooms, and their white was flushed pink by the colour on the back of each petal showing faintly through. Like all daphne blooms they glistened with a crystalline frosting, and the one cluster, on the very top of the stalk glistened and smiled at us for several weeks.

Every time we passed it we drew long breaths of its fragrance, and we passed it often, for it stood in a sheltered corner where it had full light and no wind, and sun for only part of the day.

By the time the last flower fell the top of the plant had grown out into a mass of leafy shoots, so dense that they had to be thinned. At the same time the shoot at the base of each leaf pushed out strongly, so that when spring came, Mother's daphne was a branched and shapely bush, far too big for its pot. For the last time it was slipped out, and planted in a big tub of crumbly garden loam, in its old position, and there it is still, growing as fast as it can, so that we look for wonderful things when next it flowers. We put a good layer of crocks and charcoal in the bottom, so it cannot die because its feet are wet, and very plainly it approves of the treatment it has had.

Without incomings and outgoings like these the garden can be beautiful, but they weave for it a richer personality, a fuller life. They give a whole new range of delights to gift times too. This garden is dotted with birthday gifts, and the birthdays, that might sometimes run together in memory as their number increases, retain each its separate atmosphere because of a plant belonging to it. Thus the Wilson's walnut marks a birthday for Mother; Father remembers one by the Pink Pearl Rhododendron, as by the Rose Book another, and I? — I tell the anniversaries like beads, all happy memories, yet with one here and there especially bright. One I shall take from the growing company, and show it to you, lest any should think, because I have spoken most of giving, that this garden gives more than it receives.

Gifts are always surprises in our family so there is the thrill of anticipation to add to our other pleasures. The finest gift, if one knows what it is beforehand, cannot make up for the excitement and wondering speculation with which one looks at wrapped parcels, refusing to let one's self even touch them before unwrapping, lest a touch should too much help the guessing. The pleasures of this day which I have chosen out of many days began the afternoon before, when the tri-weekly mail arrived, bringing letters and two parcels; two fascinating parcels, one addressed in strange handwriting. We gathered together to open them, Father, Mother, the Artist and I. Father cut the ties (here was no time for unknotting them), and I opened the first one, a veined bluebell from the mountains, not an intentional

Rufous Whistler

116

birthday gift, but with a glamour about it because it arrived on that day. The other parcel was larger; there was a smell of damp moss when I unpacked it, and a glimpse of nurserymen's labels.

The rock garden was young then, and as, one by one, six new rock plants were unpacked, we revelled in them together, but I most of all, for the rock garden was my peculiar pleasure. As we unpacked them and read labels, Father looked for descriptions in catalogues, and we tried to guess whence the parcel came. When, underneath them all we found a card, the pleasure was doubled by its unexpectedness. Who could have guessed that the companions with whom I had shared a mountain holiday would know this date and so recognise it?

It was too late to plant anything that night. "In the morning I'll build a cliff especially for them," I thought, and went to sleep planning it drowsily, while thought danced from it to the senders of the flowers; delighting in their thought for me; thanking them in words that they could not hear.

Then came morning, with sunshine level on the grass and dewdrops trembling in it as ripples tremble on the sea. Rejoicing in the day, I wondered if I could remember half its delights. The beauty of mornings fuses so quickly with remembered beauties that few keep their individuality, but in a warm beam of light stood a group not to be forgotten: something that belonged especially to that day. The brown and white cow who till then had had the whole green slope for her own, bent her head over twin brown and white calves. Clearly this was to be a memorable day.

When the early morning had passed — and the loving gift giving, there was more than the usual pleasantness to enjoy. The golden morning was before me: a new book to read; a rock garden crag to build.

The rock gardening came first, but was hardly begun when more gifts came. "Auntie" from the hilltop stood at the gate with her hands full of flowers. She laid the basket she held in front of me. There were wild violets in it, and maidenhair, rosebuds and alyssum clustered together, and under them, fruit from the garden, ripe and fragrant.

In the other hand she held a pot containing

an angular cotoneaster, dotted with vivid berries. In the young rock garden were no berries, and at once I imagined the many-branched little Cotoneaster horizontalis against the biggest stone. I put down the new shrub caressingly, and something else was laid in my hand. It was an envelope tinted pale gold, fastened with tawny ribbon to a spray of rose and golden flowers, and within, half wreathing the message of greeting from one who could not leave home to come, a spray of ivy, delicately drawn. I knew that the time for drawing had been stolen from a busy day. "Ivy, friendship," I thought, recalling a fragment of flower lore, "I wonder if she knows."

So the morning passed with sunlight and loving thoughts. We had tea there in the sunshine, watching butterflies among the flowers, and in the afternoon I set the cotoneaster against my big rock, "in great content." It has been there for years, making one of the happiest pictures in the garden; its bright leafed branches, alight with red berries, clinging to the stone, with, under it, violets and hairbells blossoming.

It has become part of the garden's life, where, whether we cultivate them or leave them, the plants tell the story of the seasons for each new year. By their incomings and their outgoings the garden is enriched, and we, through them, not knowing by which most, since love is in both.

Flower Painting, c.1890   Marian Ellis Rowan

The New Rock Garden

The smell of flowers,
And of the good brown earth.
And best of all along the way, friendship and mirth.

Henry Van Dyke

The making of the first rock garden was one of our biggest gardening adventures. To me it was perhaps the biggest of all. I have tried already to explain the magic that was in it, yet it remains still inexplicable and beautiful.

The New Rock Garden was begun five years later. Five years' experience of the old garden had made it almost inevitable that we should want another. It was between two trees, the oak on the right and the elm on the left, and though they were too far away to overshadow it, their roots soon found the good food packed among the rocks, and despite all our discouragements they continue to traverse the crevices and starve the plants that had been set so confidently there. Then, too, the first rock garden, which has now become the Old Rock Garden, was not well planned. Care and enthusiasm had not been able to replace experience. The ledges that had once seemed a very wonderland, and which still delighted us, were somewhat monotonous, and many of them sloped the wrong way, so that water that should have run backward under the rocks to refresh dry roots ran off in cascades over the path and the soil was parched again in half an hour. Moreover, the Old Garden was full, yet we still had rock plants needing homes.

In my first enthusiasm I had filled every crevice with plants, taking from the big garden anything that looked well among rocks. The garden was never more full of glamour and delight than on the first morning when I looked out on newly-planted crevices. Here nestled Gentian, there wild thyme, here creeping mint and fuchsia procumbens. Little sedums pressed their faces against the stones, and Rochea stood out from the clefts; there were red violets and crinkled primrose leaves, and one shy wild orchid. All that was well, but with these was Snow-in-summer, the white Cerasteum, and Polygonum with brown patterned leaves, creeping red-fruited Duchesnea, and Primula malacoides already in flower, Creeping Jenny with soft leaves, and bright-eyed forget-me-nots.

"*We* will fill the garden for you," they said, with happy goodwill, and began to do so at once. They were not to blame for their beautiful eagerness. I could not tell them that they must keep to their own strait recesses; the fault was mine for putting them there. They ran happily over the garden, no whit discouraged when I pulled up dozens of roots and cut off, first

119

handsful, then armsful, of growth. The quieter plants shrank back from them and were overwhelmed, or reached out their hands to them and were engulfed.

Thus while the old garden is still attractive it needs constant watchfulness, and there are almost daily rescues there, either from drought or crowding. So we dreamed of a new rock garden, where Polygonum and Cerasteum and irrepressible violets and forget-me-nots were allowed no foothold. They would not mind, I thought, when they had all the rest of the garden to live in.

There were more subtle reasons, too. The Artist had gone from the sleepout and the garden; shadows and many occupations had crowded some dreams in forgetfulness; new delights had arisen, but there was not the same light of morning in them, that had made the air of the Old Rock Garden radiant. For a time I thought it was lost, a little time only, for there were sunsets still, and the heart leaping up to them, and the spirit hushed to sunrises. Half conscious only of the need, I sought the old delight in old ways.

For some days I had been busy making new garden paths, and Father and I had spent a busy, happy afternoon building a big square arch for the Jessie Clark and Paul's Scarlet which grow near the front of the garden. Arch and paths alike were inspired by a longing to give breadth to the garden, which, because of its three long paths running the same way, has always looked too narrow.

John, a friend of the Teacher's school days, was with us at the time and I outlined cherished plans encouraged by the presence of a willing listener.

"And there," I said, as we reached the top of the garden where two untidy grass grown mounds against the house were miscalled lawns, "I want a terraced rock garden."

John looked at the wilderness of dandelions and tussocky fog grass and stray forget-me-nots which had come up through Mesembryanthemum which the Teacher and I had once planted to discourage it, after carrying innumerable buckets of boiling water to kill the weed seeds and only succeeding in quickening them. He showed no surprise.

"You're like my mother," he said, "always making plans." Then, feeling the comment hardly satisfactory, he added, "And they mostly come true in time, even though it seems unlikely at first. She just keeps her eye on where she wants to go, and she gets there at last."

Somewhat encouraged I outlined the great plan — "a little terrace wall right across the front, then, instead of the slope and this little three-foot path, a broad paved oblong that would give width and spaciousness to the garden as nothing else but a lawn could do."

"But, so far," I explained, "I have no stones, and it's a pretty big undertaking anyway. Still, someday ..." I paused. In a garden there are ever great things to do — "someday" — and often, more often than not, they are achieved, though it may be not just as they were planned.

Satin Bowerbird

120

Five miles away, in the hills, there was a lime kiln, and I knew that there many stones were thrown away as unsuitable for burning.

Could I buy some, I asked the manager, and how much would they cost?

He smiled at me, amused and tolerant and friendly, at once.

"Well," he said slowly, "you may have all you want for carting them away, *but*," he added, "it'll cost you a bit for cartage."

"How much?" I asked hopefully, but when he said lightly, "£1, same as we pay to have lime carted," my high hopes fell. The amount was not unreasonable, but I had not the pound, and if I had it, suggested my ever disturbing conscience, I could not spend it all on myself like that, giving myself a present that would benefit no one else.

I was once again on well trodden paths. How much ought one to spend on one's self when others are in need; how much *can* one spend and not wrong that spirit of love that we would have dwell in our hearts? There is no fixed answer to the question. One can but face it honestly for one's self, and abide by the answer of one's own love and experience, looking fairly at it each time it arises, knowing that no gift should be of duty, but of goodwill, yet better of duty alone than not at all.

So I tried to answer it, and, whether fairly or not, I know not, when the pound was actually in my hand, I was convinced, and justified the spending of it by many good arguments. So the load of stones came, and perhaps my conviction was honest, for I have not regretted it, then or since.

A generous cubic yard of stones was tumbled out of the truck on the grass near the oak tree. There were stones like chips and stones like cricket balls, there were knobby bits that could be lifted only in two hands, and many that I could not lift or move. I looked at them, handled and examined them joyfully, and dreamed more happy dreams.

Only after much labour could the terrace be begun, after how much I hardly then realised, and spring came before the least beginning was made. In the spring I left home for a while to rejoice in Melbourne with the leaves spreading on all her oaks and elms, and her wistarias cascading to the ground. In those fair gardens the rock garden was forgotten for a while. Then unexpectedly I met John. We were passing and had time for few words. He was on his way back to the Valley, where his work then lay.

"Remember about the rock garden?" he asked.

"Yes," I said, back in the Valley at the mere thought of it.

"Well," said John, a bit diffidently, "I thought you might tell me how you meant to begin, and I might do something ready for you when you come home." I was not hopeful, though I should have been, knowing John. "It will be hard work, and not very interesting," I said. "The first thing is to get all the grass off, and then cut out the terraces and wheel the soil we don't want down to the Woodland."

"Well," he said, non-commitally, "we shall see," and I waved goodbye and almost forgot what he said, knowing that it was not possible for John to reach our end of the Valley after leaving work ten miles away, before seven o'clock in the evening, and at that season it was dark before eight.

A week later I went home. John was there, washed and brushed, yet with an indefinable air of having recently worked hard, and Mother gave him supper as to one whose supper was well earned.

"Well," he said, when the rush of home talk had quietened for a moment, "I haven't done much, but I did begin the rock garden, or at least begin to get ready for it."

"He did indeed," said Mother, "come and see."

In the torchlight we saw the two mounded lawns, long the gardens' disgrace. One was grassy and as ragged as ever; the other had been transformed. The torch beam glittered over it, a bald muddy slope of yellow clay, without a blade of grass on it. In a vague heap at the bottom we saw muddy tussocks and the heads of dandelions. To a stranger it would have looked depressingly worse than before, but it filled us with high hopes.

" 'In faith that sees a waving grove'," Mother quoted, smiling.

The work was begun. The old picture which had been a failure was washed out, and the canvas lay blank, awaiting the new.

"But how did you do it," I said, knowing that there had been hours spent in hard work there. Everyone smiled and began to explain. "Reading lamps, all joined together, one into the socket of another —yours, and ours —and the one from the spare room — and the one on the tall stand from the laundry. They were so long that we were able to stand the tall one on the path and switch it on from your room. He worked till eleven o'clock last night, and an hour or two this evening as well."

I fell asleep that night planning terraces and designing a paved garden.

In the morning, at John's early breakfast, we pored over a treasure I had brought home. It was a thick grey book, with a primula blossoming on the cover, and the title boldly printed, *Rock Gardens* (including rock, paved and water gardens), by A.E. Edwards.

Father, Mother and John leaned over it while I turned the pages affectionately, and we three garden lovers talked of it long after the hum of John's cycle was lost in the distance, then Father claimed it while Mother and I fell again into the long talks that follow a holiday. The book had a story which I had told them the night before, while refusing to open it, "because it is late enough already," Mother said.

Two days before I had been in a mountain garden where lilies of the valley grow wild and gentians bloom on terraced walls, and as I left after a memorable day my hostess put a book into my hands. "I have two, " she said, "and this one is for you."

I could not look at it on the way home, but all through the day's memories of beauty and friendship and flowers that smiled in a setting where ordered beauty and wild grace held equal sway, ran the happy anticipation of opening it at my journey's end.

It was primarily a reference book wherein every phase of rock and water gardening had its place, and every difficulty concerning their making seemed answered, while the pictures filled us with delight. That evening John came again and studied it for a long time, asking questions but commenting little. Then, at the end, "We must have a waterfall," he said, and so began the transformation of my simple terrace into a rock garden with paths and waterfalls.

As John looked at picture after picture the plans expanded. There must be a waterfall with cascades, and a pool that should overflow into a bog garden; there must be bold crags and terraces and a rocky path — all this on a slope 15 ft. wide and 10 ft. deep.

I drew many plans and there were many discussions because there were so many limitations. We had only one load of stones; we must not use more than two bags of cement at most; one if it could be managed, and our space was strictly limited by the house on one side, paths on two sides, and a holly tree on the other. At last we decided to make the best design the space would permit and if there were not enough stones, leave it unfinished and hope for more.

The path that was to have been widened actually became narrowed, for the pool encroached upon it.

"First," said John, "we must dig the pond." We drew the outline in the slippery clay of the mound, and the hard gravel of the path, then John dressed himself in the old khaki suit we kept for such work and began to dig. The excavation was to be only a foot deep, so that the pond would be ten inches deep when concreted. If it were deeper we should use too much concrete; if shallower it would not be deep enough for fish and waterlilies.

By the end of Saturday afternoon's hard work the hole for the pond and bog was dug, and the form for the cement, made of two old doors and several pieces of galvanised iron, was in place.

It looked like nothing so much as a pig pen — but we were elated. The work was begun.

For a week "John's Pig Pen" disfigured the top of the garden. Muddy water seeped out of the clay slope into it, and gathered into a stagnant green pool increased by every shower. At that stage I could do nothing to complete the work except wheel barrow-loads of stones from under the oak tree to tip on to the path beside the noisome hollow.

The light garden barrow had perished during the building of the old rock garden, and for several years we had used the heavy farm barrow, which was too heavy for Mother, even when empty, and which I could hardly wheel when only half full of soil. Then I saw for the first time light iron barrows, which were being sold just then for sixteen shillings, and as the farm barrow, too, began to look old (it had to be rebuilt soon after), I made myself a present of a little red barrow that was so light that we hardly felt the weight at all. For a long time the barrow was a kind of hobby. I used it always with a sense of elation. None of us had realised till then what a hindrance the weight of the old one had been. The first time the new one was used for carrying wood I understood the feelings of a car owner who sees something threaten the mudguard's flawless paint, and decreed that thence forth a sack must be spread on the bottom if the red barrow were used for anything harder than soil or weeds.

That was before the wheeling of stones

began. Then the barrow lost its outward youth, though not its efficiency, which has not suffered despite the hard work and exposure which have earned it a new coat of paint. "Green, with a red wheel, which is the proper color for barrows," I have promised myself.

I was not quite so blind with enthusiasm that I forgot to keep a sack under the stones, but before long an ominous scrape as the barrow and I ran down the slope from the oak tree to the front garden warned us of danger. There was already a permanent bulge underneath, and from then onward the weight of my loads had to be limited by the strength of the barrow, to Mother's great satisfaction.

On Saturday afternoon I surveyed with pride my heap of stones by the embryo pond; one moment disheartened, the next delighted to see that so much wheeling had made so little impression on the heap by the oak tree. Across my satisfaction came the distant and familiar sound of a motor-cycle, and soon John was emerging from helmet and goggles, drinking tea and exchanging news with us, all at once. He pulled on the khaki overalls and rubber knee boots and came out to view the pond, the triumphant work of last Saturday. He whistled in mock dismay.

"No wonder you called it a pig pen," he said.

It was my turn to encourage, "But that won't be for long," and equipping myself with boots like his, and leather gardening gloves, I stepped over the wooden frame into green slime. It was soon baled out and the bottom scraped clean, for it was hard and nearly dry under the thin mud which we poured without compunction into that beautiful new barrow so that John could wheel it away.

The cement was ready for him, "but make it go as far as you can," I said.

"The reinforcing will take up some space, and we can use plenty of stones," answered John.

Worker.   Queen.   Drone.

I agreed reluctantly. "We must make the stones go as far as we can, too, or there won't be enough," I reminded him, and he looked amused. "You see," he said, "if I use the cement to save the stones, and the stones to save the cement, we don't get anywhere," then, hopefully, "we might use some old bricks and things like that, and any old iron that's about the place."

"Old stoves?" I queried.

"Just the thing," he agreed with satisfaction. There were two old stoves, both quite worn out, and many pieces of old iron and broken brick on the rubbish heap which had been accumulating ever since the foundations of the old rock garden were made.

We took them all down to the pond, and John began to wield a sledge-hammer in the joyful manner of an indoor worker confronted by an opportunity for justifiable destruction. In a short time the stoves were in fragments, and after I had collected the few spare parts which might be useful to us or our neighbors, I was sent to look for bricks and old earthenware, for bits of wire and iron bars, "iron bars especially — there's nothing like them for reinforcement."

The heap of rubbish grew while John mixed the first lot of concrete on a sheet of tin in the pond, turning the dry mass over and over till every grain of sand had its coating of powdery grey. When all the bricks and iron were gathered together I filled the watering can and added water little by little to his heap as he turned it over, and as he began the real work of concreting I passed him iron and bricks and wire, dipping each into water and wriggling it into place as he directed, while he worked the concrete mixture round it. Here went an oven door, there half a stove top; here a broken vegetable dish, there the flattest pieces of an earthenware bowl. Sometimes I tipped in half a bucketful of wet pebbles, and John worked them down into the mixture, making it go as far as he could.

We did not pause till the big heap of concrete was all used up. "It's useless once it sets," John explained when Mother called us to tea, so she brought out cups of cocoa, which we took gratefully.

We could hardly see when the last shovelful had gone into the form. John straightened his

back with an effort and climbed out slowly, while I pulled my wet hands out of gloves that were caked stiff with cement.

Later, fresh from the bathroom and tea, I leaned back luxuriously in a basket chair and thought of work well done, but John stood up purposefully, if stiffly.

"No use sitting down yet, or I won't be able to get up," he said. "What about joining the lights?" We remonstrated, yet gave in to his determination, and soon we were working in the gold lights and long shadows of the electric lamp.

The front edge was filled up to the level of the path, so when John mixed more concrete I cemented wet stones along the top to disguise the artificial line, letting some run out at sharp angles and pressing others back to form shallow pockets where plants could grow and overhang the water. It was after ten o'clock when we finished, and rather wearily hosed the caked mud from the barrow and cement from the shovel and carried the lamps indoors; yet we were both happy. The pond was almost done. "But the cement is finished; we need more for the bottom," John said, and my conscience stirred uneasily, as it had when I bought the stones.

Half an hour later, fresh from a hot bath, John, wrapped in Father's dressing gown, sat by a warm fire eating toast and drinking cocoa, very content. "Bed will be good to-night," he yawned, and I was almost too sleepy to reply. That night I did not even dream.

On Sunday we enjoyed the admiring comments of those who appreciated our work and the assumed derision of those who pointed out that the likeness to a pig pen was no whit diminished by our labours, and during the week I wheeled more stones. John was late next Saturday, so no work was done on the garden, but he wheeled down in the heavy barrow some of the stones that I could not move. Some had to be levered into place with the crowbar and wheeled down one at a time.

We had taken the form away from the concrete that morning, admiring our work, now smooth and firm, but there had been rain in the morning and the whole slope was soggy clay in which our exploring foot prints were more than ankle deep. More mud and water had

The

The

GARDEN LOVER

JUNE 1st, 1925

A Monthly Journal devoted to
Australian Horticulture.

SCABIOUS
(The Pincushion Flower)
Illustration by Courtesy
F. H. Brunning Pty. Ltd.

Vol. I. No. 3.   JUNE 1st, 1925   PRICE, 6D.

gathered in the pond, wisps of muddy grass stuck out of a trampled heap of clay on the path, and John looked at it in disgust.

"*What* a mess!" he groaned despondently, "and Christmas is only three weeks away. Do you suppose we will have anything fit to be seen by then?" My hopes were not damped. I had gardened for too long to be discouraged by the sight of work half done.

"Of course," I said, and began to plan the next stage of the work even while I wondered how much would be done by Christmas time. We did not work that evening. With books and plans and pencil and many papers we designed the waterfall over and over again.

The pipe supplying the front garden and the lily pool ran close to the new rock garden. "Twelve feet, joined with a union near the guava bush," said John, "and taken straight up under the holly tree to the fuchsia at the top corner of the slope, will give us a seven foot drop, but we have to take it seven feet forward as well, and keep it looking natural." I brought out photographs of waterfalls, and we chose one of those finally to supply the central idea for our fall, adapting and modifying it almost out of recognition before we had made a practicable plan. It was to begin with a miniature fall down three feet of caverned rocks into a little pool two feet across which was to brim over, falling straight, eighteen inches at least, on to a series of shallow cascades which would bring the water at last to a stone overhanging the big pond, whence it could fall uninterruptedly to the pool.

"And if we keep it just dripping," we thought, "and turn it on fully on special occasions, the pond will always overflow just a little into the bog garden, and as the bottom of the bog garden won't be concreted, it will never overflow." (John had already made a low concrete wall, an inch shallower than the outer ones, across one corner of the pond, dividing the future bog garden from it like a separate compartment.) "But that's work for another week," I said.

The next morning was soft and grey, "one of the days that would seem like Sunday, even if one did not know the date," I thought contentedly. I thought of how the Artist had loved that day above all others in the week, and was thankful for the inspiration of it, forgetting the rock garden and all our plans in other thoughts. It was half an hour later, going out to gather roses for the breakfast table, that I encountered John, whom we had thought still asleep. He was splashed with mud from head to foot. With an effort that made me hold my breath he struggled up the muddy slope with a great rock in his arms, and deposited it in a waiting bed of concrete. The slope was ploughed up by his footprints, the mattock and spade lay beside him, hardly more distinguishable than his boots from the surrounding mud; the new bag of cement stood open on the path.

He turned at my exclamation and smiled.

"I just couldn't stand it," he said. "It was such a beastly mess it nearly got me down, so when I woke up early I thought I'd get up and do something. I started at five o'clock."

He had dug out the cascades and built up the pool of five great rocks well bedded in concrete yet wholly concealing it. The top waterfall with its shadowy caverns was completed, so that one corner, finished to the last detail like an etching, stood as an earnest of what the whole rock garden was to be. No one could deride that work, whatever they might say of the still unfinished pond.

Yet warmly as we admired his work we were more concerned about John's weariness than the garden's beauty.

"How did you manage the big stones?" we asked. "Carried them," he said lightly, yet straightening his arms slowly, "I thought I'd never get the big one up. I slipped a couple of times," and he glanced at the mud on his knees.

He would not leave his work till he was satisfied that it was well done, but he came in in deep content at nine o'clock. He ate the breakfast we gave him as if he were half asleep, and we feared he might fall asleep in his bath. "Call me just before eleven," he called from the bedroom door, and we heard no more of him till then.

But at eleven he was himself again, with every hair in order and shoes polished into complete forgetfulness of mud.

"It seems like a dream," he said, looking happily at his early morning work. "I forgot all about it being Sunday morning, I was so determined to get something done."

We went indoors to other thoughts, and soon in his grave boy's voice he was reading to us all, "Laying up store for themselves a good foundation against the time to come, that they may lay hold on the life that is life indeed." The work and the play were forgotten. Across the words of that chapter of farewell I thought of the Artist with no sorrow. One does not grieve when the sure builder takes his rest confident of "life that is life indeed," and we could not know that in less than a year John must follow him, so suddenly that no taste of death disturbed his life.

The new Rock Garden, like the old, was to become a garden of memories. But no shadow touched its building during the weeks that followed, nor should touch the story of them.

There is much beside gardening to do as Christmas draws near, and John was too busy to work there again in December, but he had done the hardest part of the work, and I could make the cascades alone. Day after day, as I had time, I took happy hours from the house to play with pebbles and rocks and water and clay. There were flat rocks of various thicknesses in the heap by the pool. Overlapping some, leaving narrow channels between others, damming back water in half inch shallows, coaxing an invisible trickle into a hole where the moraine was to be, I set the stones first in stiff clay, and pouring water into the top pool till it brimmed over, watched it find its way over the cascades and into the lower pond. Almost every stone had to be rearranged many times, and mimic currents directed this way and that by pebbles stuck on with clay before the stream flowed as we had willed, but satisfied at last I broke the stones out of the clay and set them in concrete, winning John's approval when he came the next Sunday. "It really looks like something now," he said, "and you might get some more vone this week. I've sent for Ray."

Ray is his younger brother. "He is off work till Christmas. I wrote and told him he might as well be here laying the pipe to the waterfall."

"He may not want to," I suggested.

"Oh! He will want to all right," said John. "Fancy being in Melbourne when he could be here!"

During the busy Christmas week I spent one showery afternoon building a dry wall against the path at the opposite end of the rock garden

128

from the waterfall. That was another dream come true, and the afternoon passed like a song. It was a very informal wall, more like a sloping stony bank, and I set hardy little plants between the stones as I built. Stonecrops and thrift, Arabis and Aubrietia, catmint and alpine strawberries and thyme were among them. Everything grew, and is growing still, though they are not luxuriant, for it is a dry and hungry place.

Ray came two days before Christmas, bringing a friend with him. The Engineer and the Teacher were also at home, and all four, with Father directing the work, dug trenches and laid pipes and struggled with difficult connections. The work was more complicated than John had supposed, but when Mother and I went out it was nearly done.

We had our own work to do indoors, among cakes and icing and mincepies, but at noon a triumphant call took us outside to see water running lightly down the fall, brimming over the little pool to play among the cascades, and drop finally into the big pond.

On Christmas Eve Ray cleared away all the clay from the path and smoothed over the mound that was still untouched, and cleaned out the muddy pond again, making the whole not unattractive to casual visitors, and revealing to us some coherent form in our rock child still half prisoned in clay. So it remained until New Year's Day, yet with one great happening to mark the week. My Christmas gift from Father and Mother was not laid on my plate as other gifts were. It was a load of stones tipped on the grass where the others had all been wheeled away. "I brought you real pretty ones this time. Merry Christmas to you," said the truck driver. "Happy Christmas," we replied, as he drove away.

After the arrival of the second load of stones our plans for the rock garden grew faster than ever. With the Student and Teacher home for holidays and three young girls spending the summer with us, one might have thought that gardening would be at a standstill for a while, but it was rather hastened. Our guests were all gardeners, and perhaps it was familiarity with garden work and beauty that kept them flower-like. Often I would hear a subdued crunching on the path, and, glancing through

the window, see my little barrow, filled with stones being wheeled toward the pond.

"I was so quiet I didn't think you could hear," one sister would say, or the other would laugh as she tipped her load on the growing pile. "Just one more before we go to tennis," she would smile, and the Teacher and the Student dug and wheeled loads of soil for me, or the brown-haired Music Teacher, who has not yet been in this story, though she was more like sister than cousin to us all, would take housework from my hands, suggesting, "If I do this you will have time for some rock gardening later on, won't you?"

On New Year's Day they all went picnicking, leaving the house very quiet, and that afternoon I worked at the rock garden for the first time since the new stones came. Stones and soil awaited me, and with growing satisfaction I began to build terraced rock pockets on the slope near the dry wall. It was a gentle afternoon, changefully sunlit and grey. It was a fair day, I thought for the beginning of the new year, and a fair work to be doing, building and planting, with all the seasons before us for growth.

Pocket after pocket was made firm with rock and soil, each designed to hold moisture and give well-drained roothold, yet look as nearly natural as was possible in a place not naturally rocky. As it grew cooler toward sunset I gathered up little plants that had been waiting for a home, and set them in the clefts and ledges that were made especially for them. There were tiny dianthus plants, some silver and some green, that had grown from English seed, Campanula carpatica seedlings like little violet plants, succulents long kept in pots, a treasured little Cotoneaster microphylla for the highest ledge, near the steps, with golden daisies and shy primulas for crevices in the steps themselves.

I had made the steps also that afternoon, cutting out the clay deeply enough to bed the flat stones in a kinder soil. They climbed up the side of my new terrace, and across near the top to join the house steps, while part way from their summit I indicated a side path that should lead across above the pond to the waterfall. But the cliff above the pond had to be built before that path could be made, and that was work for a whole afternoon.

129

I built it during the next week, but it was rather a gentle cliff, with little of the vertical ruggedness that we had intended, for it was hard to build securely without making it slope backward.

When John came at the week-end he tried to be enthusiastic about the work.

"It would be a good idea to make it a bit steeper, don't you think?" he asked.

"But that's the best I can do," I replied.

John already had his hands on the stones. "If you moved that one," he suggested, "and put a bigger one in there ... I say. I'm making a bit of a mess. Do you mind if I pull down a bit of it and build it differently? I can move bigger stones, you know," he added, as if in apology.

"Do what you like," I said, "but remember to keep the crevices sloping back and full of soil. It's to grow things in, not just to look steep, you know."

Then I left him to the building, and before sunset he had made an imposing cliff that overhung the pond.

"Now I want a big stone for the corner," he said. "What about that one in the far corner of the old garden. It's not doing anything."

The big stone; one that I could not move, was not really necessary or conspicuous in its old position, for it had been added long after the rest had been built. I made it a bed of loam, and John set it in position, turning it this way and that till it settled naturally into place. "There!" he exclaimed with satisfaction, standing, feet apart, arms folded, on the very summit of his cliff.

That was his last work in the rock garden, but there was no more heavy work to do. All the rest I could manage, for much more than the foundation had been laid by his work and enthusiasm, and it is no wonder that we call it John's Rock Garden now.

During the late summer days when the air was soft with the promise of autumn, I built up the back of the cliff, preparing it for plants, and built a new scarp farther back, with the rocky path to the waterfall between. The building of

Photo by Peter Cuffley

the upper scarp was happy work. It was steep enough to be cliff-like, yet full of ledges and clefts packed with soil, and from the highest edge I sloped it back smoothly, broadly, to form an alpine lawn.

We read often of alpine lawns in both rock gardening and mountaineering books, and the thought of one charmed me from the first. I thought of it as a high, grassy place, with bright, small flowers, especially bulbs, pushing up through its smooth green. Instead of grass, this alpine lawn in the rock garden was to be planted with mossy creeping plants above miniature bulbs. I marked the site of my bulb groups with little pebbles. On the very crest was a scarlet anemone, on one side were English bluebells and spotted lachenalias, beyond them grape hyacinths, with autumn crocus and babianas, and on the gentlest slope my three treasured bulbs of Hoop Petticoat Daffodils. These were all we had that were small enough, even they, with the exception of Hoop Petticoats, were almost too large, but Narcissus minimus is but a name in this country, and we did not then know that English Snowdrops would grow here, where there is never snow.

Over the bulbs I set wild thyme and creeping mint, Aubretia and Phlox subulata and Campanula pusilla, with delicate bright leaves. The clefts below were set with Shamrock Pea (which would not live at all in the old garden, but is threatening to overrun the new) and Aubretia and blue and white campanulas, with one clump of our miniature liliums, which liked the soil so much that they grew nearly two feet high on their narrow ledge, and a carefully chosen cutting of cup-flower (Nierembergia) which we hoped would fall like a purple cascade over a big stone near the path. "It doesn't grow from cuttings, though you might layer it," said the generous friend who gave me the parent plant two years before. Yet I thought I would try it, for its big delicate velvet-purple cups, lovely in the garden among the roses, would be lovelier in the rock garden. The first cutting did not grow, but the second, a two-inch shoot planted in April, had become, a year later, a branched shrub ten inches high, and all through the summer the branchlets were weighed down with inch-wide flowers.

Front rock garden, 1939

After the lawn I turned to the moraine. It, too, was a dream that could not be realised in the old rock garden, for when that was built I had no more than a vague idea of the meaning of the word, though I knew of the shy flowers that would grow in it. The *Rock Garden* book changed that. In it we read, "To construct a moraine dig out about two and a half feet of soil, and make the bottom of the basin or trench slope slightly toward the front ... The lower ten inches of this basin must be made water tight ... Make an outlet in front which when closed keeps about ten inches of water, not more, in the lowest part of the basin. Now cover the bottom of the trench with about ten inches of rubble, stones, or any material that affords good drainage. Above this place another six inches or so of smaller stones ... The hollow is then filled up with a mixture of stone chips and gravel. Over this again is thrown a covering, an inch or so in thickness, formed of a mixture of ordinary garden soil, leafmould, and small stone chips ... A natural trickle of water may be led into the top of the moraine." That did not seem hard to do. There was still more than enough cement left for the bottom of the pond, and in two places in the garden we had dug out hollows designed to become moraines. The larger one was between the big

131

cliff and the lowest cascade; the smaller filled a shallow depression between the alpine lawn and the top of the waterfall. In each place we had left a small chink between the stones so that a few drops from the waterfall would overflow into the moraine.

I made the lower one first, spending most of an afternoon over it, though it was no more than a foot wide and eighteen inches long. Set in the concrete at the very bottom a glass bottle-neck provided an outlet that could be disguised behind a stone, yet corked without trouble during the summer when the waterfall could not always run. The overflow was directly over the pond, so no water would be wasted.

The top moraine was made in the same way, but was shallower, and where the alpine lawn sloped down to it I planted Aster Farrari, Farrar's "Great Bear", which had grown smaller and smaller, and quite ceased to flower in the old garden. The moraines could not be planted at once, for the soil took some time to settle, but in the meantime there was much to do. The narrow path had to be paved with stones and set with hardy creeping plants, chiefly mint and thyme, which would be fragrant underfoot. Where the path stopped short at a stone by the waterfall, a stone so broad that one could sit on it, I set Mother's clump of red bergamot, which had never been happy in the flower garden, but which grew there so exuberantly that one cannot sit on the waterfall stone without bruising it and filling the air with sweet, faintly aromatic scent.

As I gardened during the day and thought back over the work as I wrote letters at night, the rock garden began to press its way into the letters also. It was too happy an adventure to be left out, and there were many stories of plants from the old garden to tell the givers, stories both of success and failure.

There had been a Cobweb Houseleek in the old rock garden. Its cobwebbed rosettes were always fascinating, and I loved even its name. Sempervivum — always living, arachnoideum — spider-like. It was a pleasure even to say it over, and I used to visit my single rosette every morning, hoping to see signs of increase, remembering the place whence it had come, a rock garden where every ledge was a separate picture, its beauty patterned in many colours.

There the Houseleek had spread, filling every crevice allotted to it, pressing its woolly heads close into the rock. Yet mine would not grow. For a year it hardly changed, then it died. Now rich in the possession of a new rock garden not half filled with plants. I wrote to the giver and asked for the Houseleek again. "Might I try it again," I asked, and there came in reply, not one Houseleek, but twelve, all different, as well as two delicate blue-grey Acaenias.

"Each one a smile from my garden to yours," wrote the giver, whom I had almost feared to trouble, and as his smiles they are known to this day. There was but one place for them — in the low rock edging between the pond and the path, where they could have both water and full sunshine. It was empty then, but now many chinks between the stones brim with clustered rosettes of houseleek, here red, there dark green, or again so cobwebbed that they look silver grey.

Then there was the gentian. We had bought *Gentiana acaulis* when the old rock garden was made, and it had fainted and died. Then it had come to us from the mountain garden where the lilies of the valley grow, and lived for four years before it, too, died, flowerless. Yet we had a friend in whose Tasmanian garden there were beds outlined blue with gentian, so that when boxes full of its royal trumpets had been gathered and sent to the Doctor, whose home it was, none could see a gap in the blue. The Doctor had gone back to it, and he too was rockgardening. At intervals we exchanged news of our adventures. "And," I wrote now, "perhaps someday you will send me a piece of gentian from your garden. If any will bloom for us, surely it will, in the new rock garden." The carefully packed piece that came to it was so big that we could get a clump in each moraine and some in other places. They are growing well. Perhaps someday they will bloom.

Still another request I made among all those letters wherein I wrote of the rock garden because the joy of it would not be repressed. "I have lost Blue-eyed Mary," I wrote to the garden of the lilies, which should be called the Blue Garden, so radiantly do lithospermum and gentian and campanula bloom there for one who loves them. She had given me Blue-eyed Mary, and I knew no other name for the creeping plant with exquisite deep blue flowers, though I think it is a myosotis.

"Could I have it again?" I asked, knowing it for a shade-loving plant which the new garden would suit far better than the old. She sent me Blue-eyed Mary, who began to grow at once and wreathed the stones with her thin light green leaves, and later blossomed in loveliest blue, and gromwell, the lithospermum which we never call by its harsh, common name. This too had never grown in the old garden, but one of the several plants sent has taken kindly to the new. There was also a primula which grew luxuriantly for a time, then lost all its leaves and never came up again, and to me the greatest delight of all, a little plant of *Linnaea Canadensis*. I remembered Farrar's comments on this plant, which of all plants Linnaeus chose to bear his own name, and glowed with enthusiasm. It was given the best pocket in the garden, below the alpine lawn, and given the sand and leafmould that it loves, and there it grew slowly but satisfyingly for a year, then a blackbird tweaked its leafy head off, and so discouraged it that it did not make another leaf.

The planting of the moraines was the hardest and happiest work. There were so many plants that would like them and thrive in them that it was hard to exclude all but the few which might not grow elsewhere. *Dianthus alpinus*, which had grown for several years in the old garden, flowering for our delight but never increasing, was moved to the top moraine and has looked happy and healthy ever since. Blue-eyed Mary trails through a crevice in the edge of the lower moraine and smiles at herself in the water, and perhaps *Gentiana acaulis* will bloom beside her some day. The very centre of this lower moraine, the choicest spot of all, was kept for *Daphne cneorum*. This flowers in such compact fragrant bunches in English catalogues, and was so beguilingly fair and waxen in Farrar's picture, that despite all discouragements (and growers are very discouraging about its habits), I longed for it. At first it seemed impossible to get it. It is not grown here, and plants could hardly be sent from England. Seed, I found, was obtainable, but even fresh seed, sent by airmail, did not germinate. Then we found that a New Zealand nursery with which I exchanged plants listed it

in their catalogue. They sent a frail, woody bush, with many warnings about its uncertain ways, but I set it in the centre of that carefully planned moraine and sighed with content, dreaming of stronger stalks and waxen flowers. It began well, with two healthy blue-green shoots, and I fastened them down with limestone chips as Farrar advises — then went away for a fortnight, and when I returned there was no sign of the plant. A green carpet of self-sown dianthus seedlings had come up, overwhelming it, and when I cleared a breathing space round the little stalks they were dead. "Well, if *we* behaved like the violas —!" Beverley Nicholls says, to which I add, "Or the dianthus!"

Yet there have been few losses in the new rock garden, and most of the plants grow so quickly that every day brings surprises. In early spring, little over half a year after the first planting, arabis and aubretia blossomed in the wall and over the pond; the little Houseleeks were spreading eagerly, and thyme and sedums were busily covering stones, while the alpine lawn was jewel-like with many colours. Purple and heliotrope aubretias were there, and pink creeping phlox, and the fairy-like blue campanula Miss Willmott. Two clumps of golden Hoop Petticoats were lifted over them like little lamps, and the dim blue of wood hyacinths made a background for them. On the brow of the cliff, just as we had planned, stood three flaming red anemones. In some of the pockets there were early harebells, and Dianthus deltoides flung its pink curtain wherever it was allowed. Rarer flowers were not yet in bloom, but their foliage was bright on the rocks.

John saw it thus and looked at it with shining eyes. Later, the year which had begun so joyfully, and which brought us love and beauty and joy, took John from us in the midst of them all, but first he saw the rock garden in bloom.

"It was worth all the work," he said, more than content.

We remember him in that saying, and look forward, confident that whatever may come, if it is given to us to look backward, seeing clearly, we will say: It was worth all, for sorrow is no more to be wasted than joy. It too, has power to open windows in the heart, making the spirit free to a larger world.

"Nithsdale", Beechworth, c.1880

Mt. Hope, c.1900

"Dunedin", 1916

The Background of Years

God gave all men all earth to love,
But since our hearts are small,
Ordained for each one spot should be
Beloved over all.

That, as He watched Creation's birth
So we, in Godlike mood,
May of our love create our earth
And see that it is good.

Kipling

The oakboughs, unsheathed by leaves, pattern the house with shadow, and on the sunny side the hill rises gently bathed warm in sunshine to the line of trees on its brow. The whole valley is warm with content, not drowsy, but alive with light, not silent, for the long-drawn whistle of a starling cuts the air and the first lamb's cry comes over the hill.

Mother must have heard it too, or perhaps I told her when the first cry came an hour ago, for she is singing absently:

All in the April evening
April airs were abroad,
The sheep with their little lambs,
Passed me by in the road.

It is twenty-five years since we came from the house on the hill, and twenty-five years is long enough to let pass before weighing the changes, counting beauty's gain and loss in the valley. One wonders whether it would look familiar or strange to one returning who had loved it twenty-five years ago, and not seen it since. The house named "Home", which is the house on the hill, stands brown among its fruit trees, with cypresses beyond it and the blue gum and blackwood towering over them as when we lived there. The walls we can see are bare, for the pink flowering currant came down to the valley to live with us, and the red passion vine and Marechal Niel roses that festooned the verandah are cut away, but the roses bloom in Father's garden still. Grandfather's house has gone, but the orchard still blossoms down to the paddock where the cows come past to milking, and the camellias bloom where his garden grew.

To the left on the sweeping ridge beyond the cypresses the sunset trees have failed one by one, yet the two noblest remain to give a grace of earth to the sunset. Their hill that was rough and scrubby, "the bull paddock", where we were not allowed to go, is now velvet smooth with grass, and sheep crop it, waiting for their lambs. There is a new house on the ridge with sunlight dazzling on its windows and children run laughing from it down the hill, shouting to each other from road to road, for the hill road and the valley road run parallel, with the slopes between.

"Auntie's House" on the hill road, where one looks up from the oak tree, is no longer bowered in roses and lilac trees. The walls are bare and it is set in orderly gardens instead of a fragrant wilderness. Where the young trees

135

below it crown the dipping ridge, grass and sky shine through their young trunks. There scrub once clustered, round the feet of giants that are gone, but the saplings are that scrub, grown tall. There will be giants again tomorrow.

Southward there are paddocks of bush and pasture still, with the unchanged line of blue hills beyond, and the curves of the river showing dark in winter and gold in spring.

Should Three and Five and Seven years old come back, they would find changes, but they would know their home and the unchanged contour of its hills. The oak trunk that Seven spanned with her hands I cannot compass with the full reach of my arms, yet could Five and Seven and Nine years old (so old we were when we began to climb it) come back, they would know the boughs they used to climb, though their favourite seats would be grown too big for them, since last year Correa and the Teacher and the Engineer, who were those children twenty-five years ago, found the old seats big enough to hold them well.

The gardens where we grew our children's garden seeds are the rock garden now; the Artist's sleepout that is mine since he went away, with the steps and the pool and the Silver Tree beside it stand where my clarkias and larkspurs grew. The uneven line of trees on the hillside — our New Forest — with the square vegetable garden nestling low on its eastern side, is new, but the paddocks on either side are unchanged except that wires, like three silver cobwebs, dip across one, bringing electric light to the house, and on the other the deep trodden, wavering path, between Auntie's House and ours, has grown dim since others came to live on the hilltop.

The cream banksia rose that climbs by the kitchen door and wreaths the lower oak tree boughs, the bougainvillea that looks in the window and is splendid on the roof, were unborn twenty-five years ago, but the house is not changed. Such houses as this do not change. They were not built for beauty, but convenience and economy, and their builders gave little thought to breadth and graciousness. High-roofed and narrow, with white paint turning grey, the house has caught none of the beauty of its surroundings, but it lets the trees hide it, and they are kind.

Most of the trees have grown since we came here. The silver wattle, cascading almost to the ground, was a seed that Mother planted the year we came. Lucerne and stone pine, maple and chestnut and scarlet oak and the wreathed magic of wistaria all are new, but the black wattle, sixty feet from side to side, where birds nested and fragrance went forth to the valley, has fallen and died, and only the trunk, wreathed in roses and ivy, remains. Still one would know the place at once, with its line of Pinus insignis beyond the Woodland; with its orchard (though fuller and larger than it used to be) beyond the garden.

You have read the story of the garden between orchard and Woodland, and know that it has all been made in those years, and our lives knit with it. Roses and shrubs and flowers, hedge and Woodland and bush-house, rock garden, waterfall and ponds, all are new, though the arum lilies that were here before we came still bloom in the hedge, and the three apple trees in the garden. Mother's garden, along the east wall, beneath the windows, is the only one that Three and Five and Seven years old would know, for they saw her plant violets and polyanthuses, and yellow primroses, like the ones that grow there now; they looked up at the Mary lilies and smelled the heliotrope and lemon thyme and though they never saw such daffodils as bloom there in the spring; the shining double buttercups are sisters of those that she brought from the house on the hill and go back to their faintest memories.

Three and Five and Seven would find the garden a very wonderland, as other children do; and within the house are few changes such as children mark. They would know the same tables and chairs, the same coverings on wall and floor, all grown shabbier with a friendly brownness on them (though Mother has harder words for it). They would recognise the brightness of the fire that still burns three-foot logs on winter days, and the vases of flowers that are always full, though they might wonder at the way the bookshelves have grown, creeping along wall after wall. They would find their favorite books awaiting them, the *Bible Stories* and *Boys Own* and *Wonder Books* all safe but very worn, for children have been reading them for twenty-five years, and would wonder at the rows and rows of "grown up" books they had never seen, far more than would fill Father's big bookcase in the house on the hill.

Should the children come back they would know Father and Mother at once, hardly noting the changes, but the pictures on the walls would puzzle them. They would know the hushed picture of a moonlit sea, and the pencil drawing of a horse's head; they would greet with delight the new painting — new since but twelve years old — of an overflowing bowl of pansies, and that, newer still, of mountains rosy in an autumn sunrise, but they would look at the portraits and wonder. Three-year-old, who was to become the Teacher, would not know the Teacher's face, with its half-smile curving the lips and hiding in grey eyes, or the Teacher's bride, flowerlike on her wedding day. Five could not know himself as the Engineer, grave in his hood and gown, though his face is the child's face in its purpose and sincerity, or as the lover with question and faith looking out of the boy's eyes beneath the man's brow. He might pause by the picture of the Engineer's betrothed, loving its beauty and gentleness, but he would not know her whom he had not met as a child. He alone of the children does not return. He has followed John and the Artist into silence. Yet we who remain are still glad, knowing the parting is short in the face of that eternity when we will rejoice together. And his son is with us — a baby with his father's brow and his mother's eyes.

Three and Five and Seven all might wonder at some familiar line in the Student's pictured face, but they could not know him as a baby brother not yet born, baby brother with his brown face and mischievous smile, disguised as a student grown tall and grave. Seven who is Correa now, alone would find herself on the walls, for the face that looks up at her wonderingly is herself at four years old, and even to the Correa of today, who has tasted the changes of twenty-five years, it seems nearer than the modern portraits that are "such good likenesses" and so very dull.

I have tried to weld twenty-five years into a coherent whole, for yesterday lives in today, today is inherent in yesterday, and I would have you see them as one background for the

telling of the tale, which runs back and forward through them as need requires.

There are more houses in the valley than there were twenty-five years ago, more grass, and fewer trees. We have mourned over beauties lost, and sighed because of disfigurements, yet for every loss some gift was given, and the hurts have healed, coming often to other beauty. The whole is not less beautiful. The long lines of hills, the breadth of the valleys, the blue girdle of mountains that disappears behind the nearer slopes on either side cannot be changed. There are lights in the valley at night brighter than lights ever used to be, and along the rim of the hills a twinkling, like starlit foam, that becomes the lighting of streets when one draws near, though no town was there twenty-five years ago.

The forest has almost gone from our valley; it hides only in the farther gullies, but the richness of pastures, the peace of sheep grazing, of cows red and white under spreading trees, houses and gardens both cared for and loved, is a kind beauty, and it is the beauty that twenty-five years has given.

There are still patches of tea-tree where moss is damp underfoot, and scrubland where heath burns red in the ferns, and if we follow the road over nearer hills, past grassland and bracken, we can still find unspoiled waters, and plunge waist deep in undergrowth, smelling the gully scent, sinking in leafmould and delicate growth, as we go seeking the unknown, wholly content.

Our valley is not perfect; its beauty is in transition and much rests with us, since beauty must grow with the years if it is not to die. We look to the future and the work of our hands to establish it. Much has been taken, much must be given in return. Yesterday where a sweet briar had been cut from the roadside I planted a hawthorn, and where a gum had fallen set another gum.

In the schoolground, where the purple sheet of wildflowers comes no more in spring, there is a blackwood grove; where they took the gums, oaks are planted, the red box trees still stand, and, though it has lost the light of heaven that blossomed in the flowers, it is beautiful. Other places are not so fair. Round the township, with its cluster of four buildings, red box trees gave character and beauty, arching the road, framing the walls. Of these one remains. We are proud of our brick public hall, but trees were cut that it might be built, and even where there is room for other trees it stands solid and bare. Much more than money, labouriously went to its building. There were working bees when the foundations were laid, and scoops and ploughs worked in the heavy soil. The men gave time work and implements with good will; the copper was boiled for tea at noon, while wives and sisters spread dinner on the grass. The work went on to the cheerful voices of friends, and when, after milking at night, they re-gathered for the dances that were to bring money for the building, intimacies grew. Two homes on our hill count their beginning from the romance of those days, and already their children run on the road where we used to play. No one grudged labour or time for the building yet none would think of gathering to plant trees.

The butter factory, which is the heart of our district industry, is hardly less new than the hall. The old factory, which was low and white, stood beneath the tallest red box trees, and farmers with drays and strong horses came to it from all parts of the valley. The butter waggon, with its matched greys and quiet driver, took the butter to the railway six miles away. This was all part of the valley of twenty-five years ago, when an old white horse could be sent with his loaded dray to and from the factory, needing no driver, and respected by all who used the road.

The new factory is a pleasant place, with shadow and coolness inside its doors. A silent electric motor drives its churns, but the trees are gone and a red and yellow petrol pump feeds its hungry motor van. We who love the valley hope that the white and green petrol pumps which are becoming known in England may yet come here, and some trees grow in bare places.

Jean and Aunt Em's chooks

138

Harvest working bee, Tyers, c.1920

At the point below the factory where the roads divide there is room for one poplar to lift a golden tower against the dark saplings across the road, and near the walls a cherry plum could bloom.

When sleep comes slowly at night I tempt it by planting the road to the township in the darkness of closed eyes. The road comes over a little bridge, though only in winter is there a stream under it. Once manna gums spread their white boughs over the road. They were cut, though there seemed no need, but on the dream road they are planted again. Silver wattles could make the bridge beautiful, and cootamundras fill the blanks on the roadside near the low general store, with its bare fence and brown walls. Roses may yet bloom on the fence, and the hill road, that rises beyond it to end at the sunset trees, be planted again.

Three years old and Five and Seven cannot tread that road again, but the brother and sister who bear their names after twenty-five years, love it still so well that for them its enchantment does not die. Other children tread it still, and we who remember know that our enchanted world lives for them as radiantly as if their feet were the first to tread its paths.

Its inner beauty is immortal, but we would not have its outward beauty decrease, for none whose childhood clasped hands with beauty but must long for children's feet still to tread fair ways. Dreams bring enchantment to the dullest road, but if leaf and blossom and mystery do not keep the way, how shall the dreams be clothed! They may die and leave no memory, and then will the children be desolate indeed, having lost that past which nothing can hurt while it lives immortal in the heart.

The first lamb is still calling over the hill, and the sky is bright past the sunset trees. There is frost in the air, and curly-haired Fay, who plays on the hill road, is running home with a twinkle of scarlet jersey and plaid skirt, and John has left his sand castles at his mother's call from the new house past the trees. The evenings when the garden story began were no fairer than this. The same story goes on. Father is planting seeds that will be trees in twenty years; again, hearing the lamb, Mother is singing the lambs song that children love:

All in the April evening,
April airs were abroad,
I saw the sheep with their lambs,
And thought on the Lamb of God.

Epilogue

The Golden Hours

Beauty in the heart breaks like a flower.

Masefield

Daffodils and lilies, roses and orchard trees, have each their own stories, but they are all woven in the one pattern of garden growth. Its threads are of countless colours and its patterning brings us all the flowers the garden has ever known; the earth and changing seasons are the loom. And the weavers? Not ourselves, surely; three human gardeners could weave no such delight, even with thread and loom set ready to their hands. Yes, partly ourselves, by our constant and happy work; but we do not work alone, being workers together with Him who has given every tree to bear fruit after its kind, as all gardeners are, and all growers of fruit and grass and corn.

Every change in our lives had moulded in some way that living tapestry which surrounds us, and though, at different times, work and thought are directed particularly to this part or that, the whole is being woven unceasingly. When roses are in bloom the daffodil seed is ripening, with the blooming of the lilies comes the summer pruning of the roses, the planting of aster and phlox, and while the dahlias are growing the summer fruit ripens and lettuce leaves curl round crisp hearts, and we watch new wildflowers bloom.

Often, having much to do and enjoy, some part is neglected, and then there has to be a great weeding, and pruning of unruly sprays and gathering up of spent flowers, and sometimes the ground must be dug and manured and watered and planted again. There are hours, too, when we do not work at all, when we sit on the seat by the pool and watch the rainbows, when we wander the garden's length tasting its scents, the heavy fragrance of buddleia at the top of the hedge, scent of mock orange, light and delicate, the sharp fresh smell of nasturtiums in the sun, or catmint under foot. We pluck the honeysuckle flowers sucking their honey, or watch a white winged butterfly alight and lift its wings that are red and yellow when they close, as it uncoils its springlike tongue to suck nectar without disturbing the flowers we would have broken. We follow bird songs, happy when the birds are unafraid, we play with water like children, and stroke the frogs with wet fingers, or watch the bees on the oak catkins, filling their pollen sacs till they overflow and spill yellow flakes on our hands. It is sweet to taste because they have mixed it with nectar, and eating fragments of their superfluity, which is the tree's gift, its own needs

140

being supplied, we feel like guests at their table, sharing the secret both of hive and tree.

The weeds grow while we are dallying, but, good as all the work is, how would he waste his joys who only watered and weeded and planted and pruned, and did not listen to the garden's speech, carried on without heeding him, or in friendly acceptance of his company! It never changes to his mood, never stoops to him, but calls him ever to share its gladness and its growth, and above all its quietness. It is better to have weeds among the hardy flowers than to lose such gifts as those, and one cannot ask the grass as one cannot wish the flowers, to wait one's own pleasure. One might as well expect a child to play happily out of doors and come in without spot or stain, as expect the garden, watered and weeded, to remain unchanged while other work is done, nor would one wish it any more.

That is why this garden is always out of hand in some part, even when it is well tended in others, and why we are content that it should be so, for growth is life — we would not have it dead. Nor are its changes always toward disorder. For a week we may be busy elsewhere and forget the west path, then find with a quick joy that the philadelphus is white with bloom and the buddleia has called the brown butterflies. Then we tell each other of the new discovery, watching it from this side and that, stooping half absently at the same time to gather up the milk thistles that have lifted up their heads here, and the foxgloves there that had shed their bells, then turning back to the overflowing bloom. Then we find that while we were happy among the flowers the peas in the vegetable garden have rounded the pods, and the beans have come into flower.

All these are not less joys because they are renewed with every year, but rather more, because we know that for all the shed petals and fallen bells there will be other flowers, not less lovely, in other years.

There are parts of the garden that may be easily passed by, but there are others that are visited every day, or many times a day. Whether we rise early or late, and even when we are busy, it is rarely that we have not been out before breakfast time, one or two or three of us together, though we are usually alone on that

first walk of all, looking for new flowers in the rock gardens, watching the fish in the pools, and the rosebuds that morning has brought. We seek flowers that were almost open yesterday, and half consciously try to prison, as we stoop to them, that morning joyfulness of spirit that the day's work and the day's heat so often take away.

It seems in the hour of the white morning star and dewy grass as if it could not leave us at all, the robin that sings, the sunbeams that light the dew and kiss the flowers, all deepen it, yet the days are rare and memorable when it stays with us till night. On those days no blade of grass is common, no word or work meaningless, the heart rediscovers the marvel of the world, making its feast of whatever may be spread, petals of flowers, stirring of leaves, the gladness of friends met by the way, patience here, contentment there, and the unity of life in all. Then, speaking for us when our own thoughts find no words, the great writers talk with us as we work and wonder.

To me there comes often the same voice, speaking across a hundred years of that which a thousand years would not change.[1] "Then sawest thou," it says, "that this fair Universe, were it in the meanest province thereof, is in very deed the star-domed City of God; that through every star, through every grass blade, and most through every Living Soul, the Glory of a present God still beams. But Nature, which is the Time-vesture of God and reveals Him to the wise, hides Him from the foolish."

White-naped Honeyeater

[1] Carlyle "Sartor Resartus"

Calves at Mt. Hope, c.1918

These are the words of the golden day, but how often that insight which comes not rarely in the garden with the dawn, fades before mental preoccupation or bodily weariness. Happy are those who carry it in their hearts, happy also are we, weaker than they, who needing quietness often to rekindle the flame, have a garden where strength is renewed every morning.

Sometimes it is the actual work, weeding and watering, or digging in good brown soil, that we need, but there are other hours when we want only to be still, entering into the garden's life and forgetting our own.

There are troubles that the garden cannot heal, except, it may be with the help of time, but there are none that can befall one habited to the garden beauty and the garden life, which it cannot ease. There are sorrows in most of our lives, and for many, physical weariness or pain dull the edge of our happiness, but the gardener's world is not barren because of these. The joy may go from it, but the beauty stays, with the wholesome work to increase beauty, and out of this, though it may be slowly, our golden days are reborn. They come first in a moment here, a moment there, with wonderful surprise, till joy is ours again. The least seed of today will bear its flower in due season.

When we have tasted pain, and found the old beauties stay with us, and the gifts of each season come as radiantly to our heedlessness as to our welcome, until they make us glad again, we know that even if we tread a shadowed path we will not lose our way. We fear no longer, for we know that while the earth remaineth seedtime and harvest, and cold and heat and summer and winter and day and night shall not cease, and while we are alive to these, working with them as gardeners do, we will know golden days and hours of deep content. The rhythm of our own lives may falter, but the rhythm of their life endures, and steadies us until we find that we are in tune with them again.

We think on our golden days that nothing but sorrow can hurt the spirit of morning in us, yet it is not so. Sorrows are few, and it rests with ourselves to win a blessing from them, but there is no blessing in impatience or anxiety, only a sordidness that makes us unworthy of our flowers, and they may come in a moment, giving us clouds for our sunshine, drab grey for golden dreams. Yet these above all the garden can heal, and the growing things need no words to crystallise their message. "He that believeth shall not make haste." The tree knows it, content without leaves the winter through, and the daisy knows it, shaping a hundred perfect flowers under her veil before one rose-tipped petal will unfold, and the gardener is humble because they are wiser than he, and glad because no fret of his can hurt one single flower, or stay one thrush from singing. Of them is born the poet's prayer:

"God, you have made a very perfect world,
 Don't let me ever spoil it any more."

No one who has lived close to a garden could desire that flowers should fade to match his sorrow or mark his annoyance. The succession of spring and summer, the fruition of autumn and the winter rest are his consolation.

If we could not trust their law we could have no safety, and hope for no peace. The tapestry of our lives, like the tapestry of our garden's life, is woven of the stuff of every day. Of our own will is its beauty, and often its joy, but its laws are beyond our power to change, and so beyond our fear. God, who makes seed-time and harvest for our gardening, makes also seed-time and harvest for our lives, and though He gives us the planting and tending of the flowers, He made the law that governs them and us, so we know that whatever our failing it will not fail. If we plant a daffodil only a daffodil can come of it. If we broadcast thistles we must expect sharp spines as well as purple flowers. The gardener knows that law is strength, and that no law is born of chaos but of power.

We are often preoccupied with other things than these, but as from our planting and watering the flowers come to bloom, so from our joy in the garden is born the rare and golden hour, with its vision that makes every common work and word a miracle to the happy heart. That vision is not enough for the ordering of our lives. Law is pitiless unless it is the law of love, and for love we must have personality. The garden does not give us that — we seek and find it by other paths, but having found it we see it in everything, and only then do we taste the fulness of our golden days. Then is our vision the vision of Robert Bridges, who saw:

The common flowers that starr'd the fine
 grass of the wold,
waving in gay display their gold-heads in the
 sun,
each telling of its own inconscient happiness,
each type a faultless essence of God's will,
such gems as magic master-minds in painting
or music threw aside once for man's regard
or disregard;
things supreme in themselves, eternal,
 unnumber'd
in the unexplored necessities of Life and
 Love.

It is the same vision of the morning, "through every star, through every grass blade ..."[2]

[2] Robert Bridges "The Testament of Beauty"

Illustration sources and acknowledgments

Particular thanks are due to Jean Galbraith's friends who prepared works especially for this edition of *Garden in a Valley*.

Page 97 Betty Conabere, Irish Peach Apple; p. 33 Peter Cuffley, "Dunedin", The Garden as it Was; p. 66 Joan Law-Smith, Spring flowers; p. 108 Celia Rosser, Fuchsia magellanica; p. 123 Bart Sterkenburg, Gippsland Wildflowers. Peggy Shaw contributed all the wonderful small illustrations on pages 15, 19, 25, 31, 45, 55, 67, 74, 79, 87, 95, 109, 104, 114, 119, 122 and 127; black and white illustrations are by John Turner: pages 65 and 81.

Thanks also to Daisy Wood for Prostanthera, p. 112; and to Helen Vellacott for the illustrations from the *Fruitgrowers Guide* and other sources.

The Royal Australasian Ornithologists Union and the Melbourne University Press kindly gave their permission to use illustrations from the *Atlas of Australian Birds* by Blakers, Davies and Reilly. Thanks are due to the following artists: S. Haffenden, p. 96; R. Keller, pp. 64, 77 and 120; F. Knight, pp. 85, 93 and 141; R. Rehwinkel, p. 103; W. Rolland, p. 116.

All of the photographs reproduced are from Jean Galbraith's collection.

Paintings appearing in this book have been reproduced with kind permission from the National Gallery of Victoria, Melbourne; Bendigo Art Gallery, Bendigo; Castlemaine Art Gallery and Historical Museum, Castlemaine; Sale Regional Art Centre, Sale and from private collections. Gippsland Institute of Advanced Education was responsible for photographing the works from Sale Regional Art Centre.

National Gallery of Victoria, Melbourne

Marchese G.B. Nerli   1863–1926 Australian
Woman in a Garden
Oil on cardboard
43.8 x 38.7 cm.
Allen R. Henderson Bequest 1956

Ludmilla Meilerts   b. 1908 Australian
Flowers, 1946
Oil on paper on cardboard
61.2 x 50.7 cm.
Purchased 1949

Charles Conder   1868–1909 Australian
The Farm, Richmond, 1888
Oil on canvas
44.4 x 50.9 cm.
Purchased with assistance of a special grant from the Government of Victoria, 1979

Frederick McCubbin   1855–1917 Australian
Winters Morning, 1914
Oil on canvas
51 x 76.5 cm.
Presented by Jennings Industries Limited through The Art Foundation of Victoria, 1979

Tom Roberts   1856–1931 Australian
Quiet Study, c.1889
Oil on panel
24.1 x 14.3 cm.
Purchased 1958

Marian Ellis Rowan   1842–1922 Australian
Flower Painting, c. 1890
Watercolour
77.3 x 55.7 cm. (sight)
Acquired through a Government grant, 1980

Sale Regional Art Centre, Sale

Nicholas Chevalier
Surveying on the Moe, Gippsland 1876
Hand-coloured wood engraving
Published in Australasian Sketcher
34 x 31.2 cm.

Nicholas Chevalier
Fern Tree Gully
Mt. Useful Gippsland 1865
Chromolithograph
31 x 23.5 cm.

Bendigo Art Gallery, Bendigo

Marian Ellis Rowan   1842–1922
Sunflowers
Watercolour
75.1 x 54.2 cm.
Signed l. l.

Charles Wheeler   1881–1977
Warrandyte, 1908
Oil
19.9 x 27.5 cm.
Signed I.R.C. Wheeler 08

Castlemaine Art Gallery and Historical Museum, Castlemaine

John Rowell
Sliprails
Oil on canvas
25.5 x 36 cm.
Signed l. l.

A.M.E. Bale
The Pathway
Oil on board
20.2 x 20.2 cm.
Unsigned

Ina Gregory
Our Garden
Oil on board
30.5 x 22.8 cm.
Unsigned

Rupert Bunny
Still Life
Oil on canvas
46.5 x 38.5 cm.
Signed l. l.

Private Collections

A.T. Woodward   1865–1943
Interior, the artist's home, c. 1930
Watercolour
20.2 x 24.2 cm.
Signed l. l. A.T. Woodward
Coll: Deutscher Fine Art

A.T. Woodward   1865–1943
The Artists kitchen, c. 1935
Watercolour
27 x 21.2 cm.
Signed l. r. A.T. Woodward
Coll: Mr. E.F. Cusack

Plan of Garden in a Valley

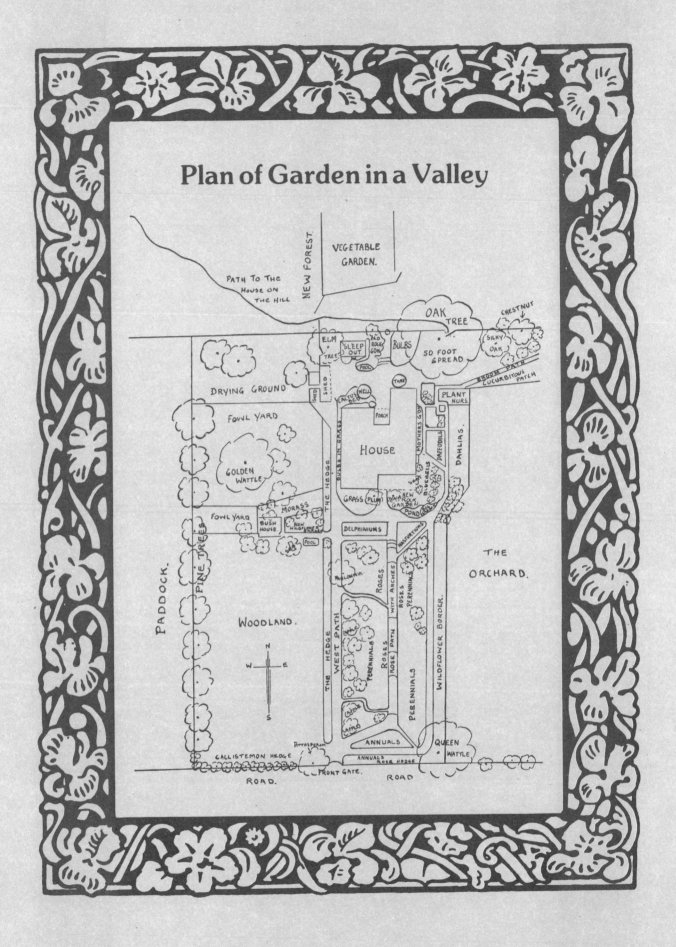